BEES IN CLOVER

by

BUD ROBINSON

Author of
Honey in the Rock
Mountain Peaks
A Pitcher of Cream

SCHMUL PUBLISHING CO.

SCHMUL'S WESLEYAN BOOK CLUB   SALEM, OHIO

Published by Schmul Publishing Co.
PO Box 716
Salem, Ohio USA

Printed in the United States of America

ISBN 0-88019-449-9

Contents

Dedication 5

Foreword 7

1: *Something New* 8

2: *Seven Confessions* 10

3: *Crossing Jordan* 15

4: *In Canaan* 17

5: *Wandering* 20

6: *Chickens Come Home to Roost* 24

7: *Fruit Bearing* 28

8: *The Fruits of Deception* 30

9: *A Few Things that Prove Depravity* 35

10: *Five Things Necessary to Get You to Heaven* 36

11: *The Marks of the Loss of First Love* 37

12: *Set Thy House in Order, for Thou Shalt Die* 40

13: *The Tree that is Dead at the Top* 43

14: *The River Jordan* 46

15: *This Great Salvation* 50

16: *Under His Wings* 62

17: *A Wall of Fire* 64

18: *Guided by His Eye* 66

19: *In the Hollow of His Hand* 68

20: *Graven on the Palms of His Hands* 70

21: *BeThe Ideal Church* 73

22: *The Two Greatest Powers* 75

23: *The Whole Lamb* 77

24: *Riches* 96
25: *Promises* 98
26: *Joy* 100
27: *Some Questions and Answers* 101
28: *My Objections to a Sinning Religion* 103
29: *The Fullness of Christ* 107
30: *The Five Crowns* 109
31: *The Moth-Eaten Garment* 111
32: *Barnabas, the Evangelist* 124
33: *The Morning Glory and the*
    Glory of the Morning 140

Dedication

I LOVINGLY DEDICATE this book to the band of faithful workers that toured the state of Indiana in an automobile in the month of April of 1916. This band of workers consisted of the Rev. U. E. Harding and wife, Rev. C. C. Rinebarger, and Miss Eunice Oakes, who is now Mrs. Kenneth Wells, and this writer. The Rev. U. E. Harding, being the District Superintendent of the Indiana District of the Pentecostal Church of the Nazarene (now Church of the Nazarene), and who planned this great campaign, was our General Manager. Rev. C. C. Rinebarger was our choir leader. Mrs. Eunice Oakes Wells was our faithful pianist and soloist. Mrs. U. E. Harding was our successful chauffeur, and the assistant leader of song. On this journey we preached to multiplied thousands of people; we moved twenty-eight times, and traveled over this state more than two thousand miles. Scores of people knelt at our altars and found Jesus, and out of this tour have come not less than twenty splendid Churches of the Nazarene, and this wonderful tour will be remembered by this little band until we meet at the marriage supper of the Lamb.

Faithfully, your brother in Christ,
—BUD ROBINSON

Foreword

REUBEN "BUD" ROBINSON (1860-1942) is perhaps the most fondly remembered holiness revivalist of his day. Born to a whiskey distiller in a Tennessee log cabin, with few of the limited advantages available to others even then, he grew to young manhood as a true son of his age. God's grace caught up with the young Texas cowboy and transformed him into one of the brightest lights of the holiness movement. His rustic background equipped him with a love for the common man, and his easy, homespun style endeared him to thousands.

This wide reputation did not come without cost, however. Early on he fell in with the proponents of entire sanctification among the Methodists, including W.B. Godbey, but the denomination was already moving in a different direction. As the Wesleyan doctrine of perfect love began to wane, its opponents moved to marginalize its adherents. Bud Robinson was caught in the net, and because he would not surrender this precious experience he found himself out of favor.

In time, though, he found a new spiritual home among those similarly ostracized. His boundless energy coupled with his folksy style produced a tireless worker, happily laboring with many different groups to encourage others to "press on toward the high calling."

Bud Robinson authored several books that are notable for reflecting his hallmarks in preaching. Laced with many colorful metaphors, they are noteworthy for marrying common, everyday imagery of the day with the highest scriptural doctrines. Whatever the subject, his books are unpretentious, easy to read and understand, even when he uses uniquely "Robinsonian" literary tools. The idea of chickens coming home to roost may seem archaic in our highly urbanized society, but we quickly understand his timeless implication of action and consequences. We may not grasp exactly why he chooses baldness to identify the bumblebee delighting in a patch of clover, but we are never in doubt of the happiness involved—or what brings such joy to the soul.

—D. CURTIS HALE

1

Something New

ONE MORNING, AFTER READING a few chapters in the Bible and having a season of prayer, I sat down and opened my Bible, and said, "Dear Lord, I want you to show me something new in my Bible today; I want to see something that I never saw before in this Book." And the Lord impressed me that He would give me something new. So my mind was directed to turn to the Book of Genesis and look at the first word in the Bible, and as I sat there and looked at it, it seemed so strange that a word with only two letters in it should start a book so great and grand and glorious as the Bible. It was the word "IN." I thought, "That is not new, because I have known that word all the time." But the Lord directed my mind to look at the last word in the Book of Genesis, and the last word was the word "*Egypt*," and He had me put the two words together and it read, "*in Egypt*." I said, "I thank Thee, Lord, for I didn't know that the last word was Egypt." Then I remembered that God's people started in Eden and landed in Egypt.

But just then the Lord directed my mind to turn and look at the first word in the Book of Exodus, and it stood out so large and beautiful—the word "now." He then directed my mind to the last word of the Book of Exodus, and it was the word "*journey*," and then my mind was directed to these four words, and they stood out before me like letters of fire— "*in Egypt now journey*." And I said, "Lord, I thank Thee once more for something new." Then He directed my mind to look at the first word in the Book of Leviticus, and it was the word "*and*." And I turned and looked at the last word of this book, and it was the words "*Mount Sinai*;" then He had me put it all together, and it read, "*in Egypt now journey and go to Mount Sinai*," for there the Lord was to give them the law.

He then had me to turn and look at the first word in the Book of Numbers, and it was the word "*and*," but I looked at the last word in the Book of Numbers and it was the word "*Jericho.*" Then the Lord directed my mind to put these words together and read it, and there it stood before me so beautiful—"*In Egypt now journey and go to Mount Sinai and receive the law, cross Jordan and take Jericho.*" But the Lord was not quite through with this wonderful discovery that He had revealed to me, so He directed my mind to the first word in the Book of Deuteronomy, and to my surprise I found this word, "*these,*" and I turned and looked at the last word of that book, and found the word "*Israel,*" and then I remembered it was "*these Israelites*" that were to make that wonderful journey from the land of Egypt to the land of Canaan. Then I said, "Lord, I thank Thee for something new." And then I remembered that not only the Israelites, but that the world itself had left the Garden of Eden and had wandered into the dark land of Egyptian bondage, but thank the Lord, as truly as He led Israel out of Egypt into Canaan, He is able today to lead every sinner from the land of bondage, into the land of perfect rest.

2

Seven Confessions

IN STUDYING OUR BIBLE we find there were seven men in the Old and New Testaments that had much to do with sacred history, made the most fearful confessions that ever fell from the lips of men, and yet there was but one of these men that received any benefit from his confession. We first notice King Pharaoh; we find his confession recorded in Exodus 10:16. His confession consisted of three words. Here is the confession as it fell from his lips: "I have sinned," and yet as fearful as his confession was and as far-reaching, and as horrible as the consequences of that confession meant to that man, yet he held on to his sins, until they put him in the bottom of the Red Sea, and though he made his confession, he received no benefit in the world from it.

We next notice a prophet, whose name was Balaam. In Numbers 22:34 Baalam said, "I have sinned." His confession was an honest one; but as truly as Pharaoh had his heart set on keeping the Israelites in bondage, Balaam had his eye on Balak's gold. But this prophet was out of God's order, and he went to curse Israel for Balak, over the protest of the Lord. But on his way, the reader will remember, God sent an angel out to meet him, and a number of times when the donkey that Balaam rode came to the angel he was turned to the right or left, and while the donkey beheld the angel, Balaam did not see it. It seems a little strange that at times a dumb brute has a greater spiritual vision than a backslidden preacher, but nevertheless this was the case with this man Balaam, and when God couldn't do anything else with Balaam, he had the dumb beast that he rode speak to him in man's voice, and then Balaam made his fearful confession. It was those three fearful words, "I have sinned," but nevertheless he kept his eye on Balak's gold until fifteen hundred years later God had St.

Peter preach Balaam's funeral; and in Peter's discourse he said, "Balaam died, the lover of the wages of unrighteousness." The reader will notice that Pharaoh and Balaam made the same confession, and yet both died sinners.

We next notice a man whose name was Achan. We read this man's wonderful history in the Book of Joshua, recorded in the 7th chapter and 20th verse. We notice that Achan had disobeyed God and had stolen a Babylonish garment and a wedge of gold, and a few shekels of silver, and he held on to these things that he had stolen until he defeated the army of Israel, disgraced the cause that they represented, grieved the the Lord, and caused thirty-six of his own brethren to be put to death, and his wife and children destroyed, and he himself was taken into the valley of Achor and stoned to death. But we find that Achan had made the same fearful and awful confession that Pharaoh and Balaam had made. He said, "I have sinned," but he held on to his crookedness until it damned him. Beloved, when will we learn a lesson from these fearful and awful consequences of holding on to sins until they wreck and ruin precious and immortal souls?

The reader will see that these three men made the same confession and neither of them received any benefit. My judgment is that each of them made an honest confession, but nevertheless each man held on to the sins he had confessed until they destroyed him.

We will next notice King Saul. In 1Samuel 26:21 Saul said, "I have sinned," but he held on to his disobedience, and carried jealousy in his heart and laid plans to murder another man, and so grieved God that God would talk to Him no more. The reader will notice that Saul made the same confession that the other three had made, but nevertheless, don't forget, beloved, that Saul held on to his sins, though he had confessed them, until he fell on his own sword and ended his own life on Mount Gilboa. He was Israel's first king; he was chosen over God's protest and had a good start, but a fearful and awful ending. He held on to his sins until it was too late to get back to God.

Our next man that made this fearful confession was a man whose name was Shimei. We read of him in 2 Samuel 19:20. Shimei said, "I have sinned," but he held on to his sins, and his crookedness, and his skullduggery until he was finally put to death by King Solomon, and died in disgrace, and left a blotch on Israel. Although his confession was honest, he did not forsake his sins, and they finally destroyed him, and I am convinced that every reader of this page can call to mind some friend or neighbor, or maybe some relative, who to their knowledge have made honest confessions time and again, but yet never did forsake their sins, until finally their sins destroyed and damned them.

We next notice probably one of the saddest characters described in the Holy Scriptures. This is Judas Iscariot. We read in Matthew 27:4 these same three fearful words, "I have sinned," and yet while Judas confessed his sins, he held on to the thirty pieces of silver, until Christ was captured, and tried before Pilate and Herod. He had worn the crown of thorns and purple robe; He endured the Roman scourge, He had been beaten and was spit upon, mocked, and hissed as He staggered under the cross, and was finally nailed to the cross; the earth had reeled and staggered, and darkness like a nightmare had settled down over the Judean hills, and the Son of God had begged for water and had been refused, and could only have a cup of gall, and hardened sinners had wagged their heads and said, "Truly this was a righteous man," and yet, beloved, up to this time Judas is still holding on to those thirty pieces of silver. What a horrible thought, to think that a man of good intelligence will hold on to that which is perishable until he loses that which is eternal. Yet we find that Pharaoh, Balaam, Achan, King Saul, Shimei, and Judas Iscariot, all six, have done that very thing.

We next notice the prodigal son. This is the only man out of the seven who confessed and received any benefit. We read in the 15th chapter of Luke and the 18th verse, the words of the poor prodigal, "I have sinned." But the prodigal not only confessed, for no sooner had he made his confession to himself and the hog pen, he resolved to arise, retrace his steps, and go back to his father's house, and make the same confession there that he had made in the hog pen. So we hear him say, "I have sinned, but I will arise and I will go to my father, and I will say to him, 'Father, I have sinned against heaven and before thee; I am not worthy to be called thy son, make me to be one of thy hired hands.'" Thank God, he left the hog pen, and took up his lonely march, clothed in rags, facing a wrecked life, carrying a guilty conscience, but headed in the right direction. And, beloved, think of this, we next read that his father saw him when he was a great way off, and ran to meet him, and when the father met the wayward boy he fell on his neck and kissed him. The poor, dirty, ragged boy, undertook to make the same confession to his father that he made in the hog pen, but his father kissed him and pulled him to his bosom, and, bless God, the past record of the prodigal son was blotted out. What a wonderful picture of God's love! Here we see such beautiful marks of the love of God, as He deals with a penitent soul. We first notice the father ran to meet him. No man can read of the old father running to meet this returning prodigal and fail to see the wonderful interest that the father felt in his heart for that beloved boy. In the second place, we can see the old father's arms around his boy, and he pulls him to his bosom. You can just see the old white locks hanging over the boy's shoulder, and the tears as they trickle down over the white beard. In the third place, we see the old father planting the kiss of reconciliation on the face of his boy. There the father and the son were reconciled. In the fourth place, we see the old father putting a beautiful robe on this returning boy. Beloved, there is the robe of righteousness that our heavenly Father will hand over to every returning prodigal. This is a beautiful gospel robe. It meant the dark past was blotted out, the future before him was shining bright. But, in the fifth place, we notice that the old father had them to bring a pair of shoes and put them upon his boy. Thank God, here we see a splendid pair of gospel shoes, and now the poor prodigal that was barefooted is "shod with the preparation of the gospel of peace."

In the sixth place, we notice that the old father put a ring on the hand of this boy. He now has his kiss of reconciliation, the beautiful robe of righteousness, the splendid gospel shoes, and just think of this, it was sealed with the father's ring, as it was placed upon the hand of the prodigal boy. Now we notice the seventh thing that took place. Listen now, you will hear the old father testify. Here is his testimony. He said, "This, my son, was lost, but he is found; he was dead, but he is alive forevermore; I have received him safe and sound." A spiritually minded man can see that all of the above marks of these wonderful steps in divine things makes up a clear cut case of salvation from sin. But we not only believe in the first work of grace, but, with John Wesley, believe in the second blessing, properly so-called. And now we want to prove to the reader that though this young man had received so much, there was still room for a second blessing, for the old father now gives the command, "Let the fatted calf be killed, and let us make him a feast." And the next time we see the old boy he not only had the kiss of reconciliation, and the robe of righteousness, and the gospel shoes, and his diamond ring on, but, bless your heart, he had beef gravy all over his face, and the music was rolling, and the old boy was dancing, and they were making merry.

Now, beloved, don't you see that after this man had left the pig pen and had made his confession, and had received the kiss, and a robe, and a pair of shoes, and a ring, and had received his father's testimony that he was found and was alive, yet up to this time the fatted calf was still kicking up his heels in the barnyard, showing that the boy didn't get the second blessing until after he had gotten the first.

And there is another point right here that can be noticed just at this time; while the music and dancing was going on, the elder son returned from the field, and raised a fuss with his father, and got mad, and would not go to the feast. His old father went out and entreated him, but the last account we have of the elder brother he was not in the banquet hall, but was on the outside with a spell of anger and sulk. Doesn't that look a great deal to you like the holiness movement of the twentieth century. How many times have the readers seen some poor wayward boy get gloriously converted, and some few months later get powerfully sancti-fied, and then just see the elders of the church, who ought to be at the feast, taking part and eating tenderloin steak and dancing before the Lord, but, how sad, they turn away and begin to fuss, and accuse their heav-enly Father and call the returning prodigal hard names. How many times I have seen the story of the prodigal son fulfilled; they are well nigh without number. But, thank the Lord, the old prodigal sure did get the goods, and no make-believe about it. I have always admired the man that will make his confession and go to the bottom in order that God may bring him back to the top, for after all the way up is down. Praise the Lord from whom all blessings flow!

3

Crossing Jordan

MY DEARLY BELOVED, I believe it would be interesting to you and me to study together for a little while the crossing of the Israelites from that dreary stroll in the wilderness through the beautiful River Jordan, over into the lovely Canaan land. We read in Joshua 3:17, "And the priest that bare the ark of the covenant of the Lord stood firm on dry ground in the midst of Jordan, until al the Israelites had passed clean over Jordan."

First, we want to notice that there was no crossing of the Israelites until they had broken camp. We see that a man must break camp and leave the old crowd before he can cross Jordan and get into the land of Canaan.

Second, we notice that the water did not divide until the feet of the priest had struck the brim of the water. It is just so with us; we must start by faith, and faith alone.

Third, when their feet struck the brim of the water the waters were dried up and the upper waters were backed up.

Fourth, while the priests were standing on the dry land in the bottom of the River Jordan, God commanded Joshua to command the people to take twelve stones, and pile them up in the River Jordan. This was to be a hidden secret testimony that was hid from the eyes of man. For the Lord knew that the waters would soon cover the twelve stones, but it is a fact that every man that crosses Jordan, has a beautiful hidden testimony that is hid from the eyes of a grinning, giggling, hateful, scornful world.

Fifth, they were to take up twelve stones from out of the bottom of Jordan and put them on their shoulders, and carry them up and pile them on the banks of Jordan. This was to be a public testimony for this pile of stones on dry land was where everybody could behold it;

so that proves that every man is to have two testimonies; one hidden and the other public. All this was to prove they had crossed over Jordan and were now on the Canaan side of life.

Sixth, they struck camp over in Canaan and it was known to all the dwellers in the land that the Israelites were now in Canaan, and in possession of their own country.

Seventh, when the Israelites crossed the River Jordan God seemed to draw a line through the river, and the water above the line backed up, we read, "very far off to the city of Adam," and the little city on the banks of Jordan that was called Adam was overflowed and drowned out, and the city has never ben rebuilt, and so it is with us, when we make the second crossing the city of Adam in us is destroyed with the baptism of the Holy Ghost and fire, and it is God's will and plan and purpose with us that that old city shall never be rebuilt. Well, amen, thank the Lord! I remember when the city of Adam was destroyed in me; I felt the fire burning, and I saw the smoke curling, and I saw the Devil running, and I was leaping in the air, praising God that the "Old Man" was dead, and I went to my own funeral, and there wasn't but one mourner there, and that was the Devil. And while the Devil howled and growled, and said it wouldn't last, and it was all a delusion, and there was nothing to it, and nobody had ever had it, and that I couldn't live it, I sat down and laughed and cried, and praised God that I had traded off nothing and gotten everything. From that day to this, I have been as happy as a baldheaded bumblebee in a hundred acres of red top clover.

In my visions I have seen rainbows, and orange blossoms, and clover fields; I have heard the birds singing, and have seen bees sipping honey from the clover blossoms, and I have had a beegum in the backyard of my soul that I haven't robbed this spring, and my bees have swarmed every week for thirty years, and my pancake tree is loaded to the waterline and my honey pond is deep enough to swim in and I don't call the Devil "colonel" any more; I just call him Devil, for he is one, and he knows he is, and I won't take it back. Amen! I ring off right here.

4

In Canaan

DEAR SAINTS: I would be glad to preach to you a few minutes about the wonderful things that I have discovered up here in the land of Canaan. This is truly a goodly land, and I read in Joshua 5:11-12, "And they did eat of the old corn of the land on the morrow after the passover, unleavened cakes, and parched corn in the selfsame day. And the manna ceased on the morrow after they had eaten of the old corn of the land; neither had the children of Israel manna any more; but they did eat of the fruit of the land of Canaan that year."

The reader will now remember that Israel first had manna from heaven given them as it is described beautifully in the 16th chapter of Exodus, and the forty years that they wandered in the wilderness their manna never ceased. But here we read that after they had crossed Jordan and struck camp in Canaan, and had eaten of the old corn of the land, the manna ceased. And let the reader remember this wonderful statement, that God said, "Neither had the children of Israel manna any more." So, beloved, there is such a thing as getting into the land and living on the old corn and fruit.

We next notice that the Lord magnified Joshua in the sight of all Israel. Up till now Joshua had been the servant of Moses; but now, as Moses was taken to his heavenly reward, Joshua was to become the leader, for Joshua was to take the place of Moses, for we read that Joshua means "savior." We read that Moses for forty years stood between Israel and God, and that Moses carried the Israelites in his bosom, as a mother carries her child. For anyone to take the place of Moses he must truly be a remarkable personage; so Joshua was to be both a leader and a savior to the Israelites. We read in Deut. 34:9 that "Joshua the son of Nun was full of the spirit of wisdom; for Moses, the servant of the Lord, had laid his hands upon him." We now notice several things that Joshua was to do.

He was to re-establish the rite of circumcision among the Israelites; for when they disobeyed God at Kadesh-barnea, and turned back into the wilderness, and became a band of wanderers, they lost the rite of circumcision, and for forty years, they failed to circumcise their children according to the commandments that God gave to their father Abraham. Just so when any man backslides, he loses that which he had received and for forty long years they wandered without the rite of circumcision in their camp. We read this remarkable statement: "For their young ones had not been circumcised." Right here let me add a wonderful statement that is often made by the Rev. Will H. Huff. He says that God desired to make Israel a nation of priests, and they disobeyed God and made a nation of peddlers.

Second, we read that Joshua re-established the Passover, for in their traveling they had lost that also, they were without the rite of circumcision and the Passover, and all this goes to prove to us that nothing is so dangerous as to disobey God and turn backward when God says, "Go forward." For the rite of circumcision and the Passover were the two beautiful distinguishing marks between the Israelites and the heathen about them.

Third, we read that God said to Joshua, "This day have I rolled away the reproach of Egypt from off you." Wherefore the name of that place was called Gilgal, which means, roll, and the reproach of Egypt being rolled away they were happy and free. No longer were they to work under the lash of the taskmaster, no longer were they to gather straw and make brick, no longer were they to work in the slime pits. They were out of bondage, they were out from under the dominion of Pharaoh; they had safely crossed the Red Sea, they had seen their enemies buried under the red sand; they had the manna from heaven, they had the golden pot, which represents a pure heart filled with manna from heaven. They had finished their wanderings in the wilderness; they had seen the River Jordan divided, they remembered the pile of stones in the bottom of the river, which God commanded them to pile up to remind them that He had brought them through the divided waters of Jordan. They saw the heap of stones on the bank that God commanded them to pile there as their public testimony. They were now eating parched corn and grapes and pomegranates, and the good things of the land of Canaan, for the reproach of Egypt had been rolled away.

They were now ready to take up their march around the walls of Jericho, but at that time as Joshua was walking around the camp of Israel, behold, he met a man with a drawn sword in his hand, and Joshua met the man face to face and said, "Who art thou, have you come to fight for us or have you come to fight against us?" The man said, "Nay, but as the captain of the Lord's host, am I come." Joshua realized that a heavenly messenger stood before him, and Joshua fell on his face, and said, "Take the lead, behold, I will follow thee," and Joshua woke up to the fact that he had a leader in the person of the Lord Jesus Christ. And from the days of Joshua until now, every man that is willing to be led will find the leader, and every man that is willing to be taught will, find the teacher, and every man that is willing to obey will find a commander.

5

Wandering

WE HAVE JUST NOTICED the Israelites entering Canaan and how happy they were, but we might do well now to stop and consider a few minutes the real condition of the great multitudes in the churches who have refused to go into Canaan, and for a scriptural text we might use Deut. 1:19, "And he came to Kadesh-barnea." We have heard it said by scholarly gentlemen, that Kadesh means "holiness," and Barnea means "wandering." And we have often noticed in our short life church members who come to the light of scriptural holiness and refuse to go in and receive this beautiful experience, and like Israel of old, they turn back and begin to wander, which in a sense means milling; that is the Israelites between the crossing of the Red Sea, and the crossing of Jordan, spent forty years going round and round, crossing their trails and often camping on their same old camp ground. So it is with tens of thousands of the people today. They remember well when they were converted, and they came up to a great holiness campmeeting, and had the light, and the Devil said, "Not today," and they turned back and they are not as near the happy land today as they were ten years ago. Beloved, it is a dangerous thing to refuse to walk in the light when God throws it across your pathway.

But as they are very active in church work, the Devil tells them they are making progress. The Israelites, we remember, did not stop and sit down; they traveled all the time, but at the end of forty years they were no nearer Canaan than when they started. The Israelites had many good times before they got to Canaan. Just after they crossed the Red Sea they had a great hallelujah praise meeting, led by Miriam. Here we see the Salvation army lassie for the first time. Miss Miriam played the tambourine, and danced before the Lord, and sang, "The horse and the rider hath he thrown into the sea." This is a typical Salvation Army meeting, for the Army has been the only people in our country that took all the good tunes they could gather up and put their own words to them, and sang them to the glory of God. We see Miriam making her song as she went. After the great praise meeting the Lord led them over the hills toward Canaan, and they struck camp in a place called Marah. The word Marah means bitter, for they had a bitter well to drink out of, and when they cried, "bitter, bitter, bitter," Moses cut a limb off of the tree, and threw it in the well, and it sweetened the water. From this we find that a Christian doesn't run long after he is converted until he has to drink out of a bitter well. This is his first real test, and God tests every convert.

From Marah Moses led them over the hill to another camp which is called Elim. Elim is very different from Marah. At Elim they found twelve wells of pleasant or sweet water. They also found threescore and ten palm trees. Here we notice some marks of a Christian experience. There are twelve in the year and there were twelve sweet wells. We ought to drink out of a sweet well every month in the year, and there were threescore and ten palm trees, and the Lord said your allotted time is to be threescore and ten years, so we see we have a sweet well for every month and a palm tree for every year. The historians tell us that the palm tree is the most useful tree in the world, that it has been put to three hundred and sixty-five different purposes. The palm tree is so useful and represents the Christian life in such a remarkable way that our beloved Brother W. E. Shepard has written one of the most beautiful books I have ever read on "The Palm Tree Blessing. "We find we have three hundred and sixty-five days in the year, and we notice now that we have a sweet well for every month, and a palm tree for each year, and something useful for each day in the year. Well, beloved, at a glance you can see that the above statement will knock in the head the idea of being religious on Sunday and then crooked on Monday. But real salvation will make us just as religious on Monday as we are on Sunday. But as great and as glorious and as beautiful as these experiences are, they were all this side of the land of Canaan and we have often heard people say they have been blessed a thousand times therefore they didn't believe in the second blessing, but beloved if you have received a thousand blessings, surely you ought to be willing for us to have two—the first and second—and then, according to your testimony, you are still nine hundred and ninety-eight ahead of us, so I don't see why you should set up a howl because we have received two. But yet, beloved, like the Israelites, these people that have been blessed so many times, and had a shouting spell today, are liable to have a wandering spell tomorrow. For you will remember that as great as their sweet well and palm tree were, they were by no means in the land of Canaan.

Another beautiful experience the Israelites had before they got into the land of Canaan was seen in this beautiful fact: they received manna from heaven which was white like coriander seed, and the taste like wafers made with honey. This beautiful manna was a type of the witness of the Spirit, for we read that it was angel's food, and sent to the Israelites from heaven. But from the reading of the book we note that at times they had trouble with this manna. They seemed to put some of it in a crock, or wooden bucket, or iron kettle, and it soured, and the worms got in it. The reader will notice that the trouble was not with the manna, but with the kind of a vessel they were keeping it in. So it is with the justified man. He could not have any trouble with his justification, but he is trying to keep it in an unsanctified heart, and we have often heard a man say that he is a poor weak worm of the dust, and when he would do good, evil was present and hindered him. Oh, beloved, the worms have gotten into his manna. But God commanded Moses to command Aaron to gather up an omer of this manna and put it into a golden pot, and it would keep sweet to the rising generations, that the nations round about them might see the bread that He had fed them on in the wilderness. This golden pot and heavenly manna are a beautiful type of full salvation. The golden pot is a type of the sanctified heart, for gold stands for purity, and the manna is a type of the Holy Spirit, so there is a purified heart, filled with the Holy Spirit. God gave them this that they might understand what beautiful things He had for them later on, and what rich treasures he had for them reserved up in the land of Canaan.

But after their sweet well, and palm tree and golden pot and manna, they did all of their wandering. They became restless and dissatisfied, and discouraged, and disheartened, and wanted to go back into Egypt, and get onions, and garlic and leeks, and cucumbers, all of which are a type of an unsanctified heart. We have seen the wanderings of the Israelites so wonderfully fulfilled and carried out by the American church members that today the average life of the average church member is a complete repetition of the wanderings of the Israelites.

6

Chickens Come Home to Roost

IN THE BOOK OF Exodus, the first chapter and 22d verse, we read that Pharaoh commanded Moses to be drowned in the River Nile. But Moses, being God's favorite child, and a child that was predestined to do a great work for God and for God's people, God's eye was on this remarkable boy, for the reader will understand that this boy Moses was to give the law to the world. And when Pharaoh laid his plans to drown Moses, God was much displeased with Pharaoh's plan, and we read that God had Pharaoh to take Moses and educate him until he was taught in all the wisdom of the Egyptians, and he was the most mighty man intellectually in the whole nation. After the education of Moses was complete we read again in the Book of Exodus, at the 14th chapter and 27th verse, that God had Moses to drown Pharaoh, so we see that the very kind of death that Pharaoh planned for Moses, God and Moses planned for Pharaoh. So my beloved, don't plan something evil for your neighbor, for it is possible that the very death that you plan for your neighbor, God will allow to come to you—for "Chickens come home to roost."

Hung on His Own Scaffold

Again we read in the Book of Esther, in the 5th chapter and 14th verse, that Haman had a gallows built fifty cubits high, to hang Mordecai on. Mordecai was a holiness man and was a man with such spiritual insight that God's peculiar love and protection were thrown around this remarkable Jew, and he was a man of great wisdom and piety. While Haman, sorry to say, had neither one. But we see that the plans of Haman were all defeated, for God's hand was with the holiness man and against the holiness fighter, and so we read again in the 7th chapter of Esther and 9th verse that Haman himself was hanged on the same gallows that he had erected to hang Mordecai on. This is another proof of the fact that "chickens come home to roost." The reader will remember that Pharaoh planned to drown Moses, and God had Moses to drown Pharaoh; and now Haman builds a gallows to hang Mordecai on, and God planned and worked the plan successfully, and to the surprise of everybody in Babylon, Mordecai hung Haman on the gallows that Haman built to hang Mordecai on.

Caught in Their Own Trap

We read again in the opening of the 6th chapter of Daniel that all the presidents and governors and princes had laid a plot that was very dirty and subtle. This scheme was so subtle that even the king was deceived by it. This plan was to catch Daniel, the only holy man in the city of Babylon at that time. These holiness fighters and holiness haters and God-rejecters pretended to be great friends of the king, and now they rush to the king as though they were much interested in him and his affairs, and said, "Oh, king, live forever." Then they notified him that all the governors. and princes, and presidents desired to bring great honor to him, and now they said, "King, we want to pass a decree, and sign it with your ring, which is according to the Medes and Persians, unchangeable, and this plan is this: That for the next thirty days no man shall ask a petition of any God except thee, oh, king." And the king, being completely caught with their guile, never once mistrusted their sincerity, but was blindly led into their scheme, passed the decree and sealed it with his ring. Here is their piece of deception: And the decree was this, that if any man asked a petition in the name of any other God except the king, he was to be cast into a den of lions. Now, reader, doesn't that look a good deal like the plans of a holiness fighter of the twentieth century? Where is there a man of any traveling experience that has not seen and heard just such dark, muddy, secret, and mysterious plans worked out to get rid of some good holy man or woman because of their beautiful testimony?

But, thank the Lord, we read that when Daniel knew that the decree had been signed, he went into his room, as he had been doing before, with his windows open toward Jerusalem, and on his knees he made his petition to Almighty God, three times a day, just as he had done before. And behold, the governors, and princes, and presidents caught Daniel on his knees in prayer, and then they raised a shout and said, "We've got him, we set the trap for Daniel, and he is caught in it, for the decree can not be changed, therefore Daniel must go into the den of lions, and we will get rid of this disturber of the peace of Zion." And it was made known to the king that Daniel was caught in prayer, asking petition from God instead of him. At that time this subtle, black, mysterious, unbelievable, unthinkable scheme of the governors, and princes, and presidents was made plain to the king. He saw that they had not only caught Daniel, but they had caught him, for he loved Daniel, and he never even suspicioned that their plans were to catch Daniel.

So we read that he labored until the going down of the sun that Daniel might be delivered. But as the decree had been signed and sealed with his own ring, the decree could not be changed. Therefore Daniel must go into the lions' den, and into the den of lions Daniel went. But, bless your heart, we read immediately following that God had sent an angel, and had locked the lions' mouths, and so Daniel spent the night in the lions' den, and the king was so sad that he had all music, and dancing, and feasting suspended for the night, and at break of day he hurried to the lions' den, and cried with a loud voice and said, "Oh, Daniel, has thy God delivered thee?" And Daniel shouted back, "Oh, king, live forever; the God that I serve has delivered me," and Daniel came out of the lions' den without a mark on him. Then we read that the king had the governors, and princes, and presidents brought, and had them cast into the den of lions, and we read that the lions had the mastery of them and before they ever reached the bottom of the den their bones were broken. So we see again that "chickens come home to roost."

Beloved reader, don't forget this remarkable piece of history; keep it clear in your mind, that the death that Pharaoh planned for Moses, the same death came to Pharaoh; the death that Haman planned for Mordecai came to Haman, and the death the governors, princes, and presidents planned for Daniel came to them.

And the Dogs Licked Up His Blood

We want to notice again that in Genesis 9th chapter 6th verse God said, "Whosoever sheddeth man's blood, by man shall his blood be shed." God said it was because man was made in the image of God. As far as I can find, this is the only reason why one man shouldn't kill another, because God said that man was made in His image. And that proves that any being who is made in the image of God is not to be killed by man, and now we will see that these Scriptures were fulfilled, for we have just read that "he that sheddeth man's blood, by man shall his blood be shed." We read in I Kings 21st chapter, that Ahab and Jezebel wanted to buy a vineyard that belonged to Naboth, and Naboth did not desire to sell his vineyard, and refused to take their offer, whereupon Queen Jezebel laid a plan whereby they might get Naboth's vineyard. She notified the leaders of Israel to proclaim a great feast, and while the feast was on, to prefer charges against Naboth, as though he had committed some bad crime, and take him out and stone him to death. They stoned him at the pool of Samaria, and the dogs licked up his blood, whereupon, Jezebel called Ahab, and told him to go down and take possession of Naboth's vineyard, for said she, "Naboth is dead, and is not alive," and God sent the Prophet Elijah to meet Ahab at Naboth's vineyard, and Elijah said, "Behold, in the same place that the dogs licked up Naboth's blood, shall the dogs lick up thy blood, even thine." And we read that Ahab was killed in battle, and brought back to the pool of Samaria in a chariot, and that the blood was washed out of the chariot, and the dogs licked it up where they did the blood of Naboth.

Then Elijah declared again that the dogs would eat the flesh of Jezebel, we turn and read in II Kings, the 9th chapter and the 36th verse, that when Jehu was anointed king and went into Samaria and had a great feast, that Jezebel dressed up and looked down from the upper story at the young king. He commanded his servants to go up and pitch her out of the window head foremost into the streets and kill her, and when his dinner was over, he told the servants to go and bury her, but behold the dogs had eaten her up, and nothing remained but her head and feet and palms of her hands. Then Jehu said, "This is the word of the Lord, that the dogs shall eat up Jezebel."

7

Fruit Bearing

WELL, AMEN! GREETINGS TO the reader from John, the 15th chapter. As we study this remarkable chapter we study it under the rule of four. First, we find a branch with no fruit on it at all. This is a branch but no fruit. Second, we see a branch with some fruit. That is better than no fruit, but it is the poorest condition that a Christian can be in to live at all. Some fruit is the lowest standard that God will put up with. Third, we see a branch with more fruit on it. That is better than some fruit, but just how much better we are not told. We see that more fruit was not the best that God could do and that He is able to bear "more fruit." More fruit, as good as it is, is not God's plan, for we see the fourth branch, and behold it has much fruit on it. And that is coming up to the Lord's standard.

Now let the reader run back over these branches, and see the difference. First, no fruit; second, some fruit; third, more fruit; and fourth, much fruit. No fruit is a dead branch; some fruit is a converted man; more fruit is a holy man, and the branch that bore much fruit is the holy man fertilized and pruned and sprayed and irrigated and at his best for God. He is in the best soil, and in the best climate, and in the best condition that a soul can be in this present world. And that makes him bear much fruit. And it is the branch that bears much fruit that brings glory to God. For Christ said himself , "Herein is my Father glorified, that ye bear much fruit. So shall ye be my disciples."

Now, here is the secret of bearing much fruit, and it is in the words of Jesus: "If ye abide in me, and I in you, ye shall ask what ye will and it shall be done unto you."

Dearly beloved, we want to see a few things from the thirteenth chapter of Matthew's Gospel. First, we want to notice the sower and the seed. We notice that John, the fifteenth chapter, worked under the rule of four, and we see here that the thirteenth of Matthew works under the same rule. Second, we see the sower gowing forth to sow. And when he sowed, some of the seed fell by the wayside, and behold the fowls came and devoured them up, and he sowed the second time, and the seed fell in stony ground, and they brought forth no fruit, and he sowed the third time,and the seed fell in the thorns and thistles, and brought forth no fruit, and he sowed the fourth time, and the seed fell in good ground, and brought forth fruit some a hundredfold, and some sixtyfold, and some thirtyfold; so here we have four sowings. We see that the first three sowings were lost, but the fourth sowing was successful, and as far as we can see none of the fourth sowing was lost, but we see that only one-third of the fourth sowing comes to perfection, and brought forth a hundredfold, and one third came two-thirds of the way, and brought forth sixtyfold, and one-third only brought forth thirtyfold, which is less than one-third. If it had been us doing the talking instead of the Lord, we would have said, thirtyfold, sixtyfold, and a hundredfold, for as we are on the bottom we always begin at the bottom and go up, but as God is at the top, He begins at the top and goes down, but God's standard is perfection, and He must begin with the standard high, and He keeps it high, and God was never guilty of giving the world a low standard. And we have gotten all the low standards after we backslid. The seed that brought forth a hundredfold is the seed that caught the eye of God, and that proves that all of God's plans are laid for the purpose of bringing us to perfection, and the man that lives below his best is not pleasing the Lord the best.

8

The Fruits of Deception

IN THE TWELFTH CHAPTER of the Book of Genesis we read that Abraham said of Sarah that she was his sister, and in so saying he misrepresented the facts, although she was his half-sister, yet she was his wife. We will notice now the outcome of this case of deception. For in the 20th chapter of the same book he got into another hard place, and said of his wife the second time, "She is my sister." You see he misrepresented things twice, and we see the effect of the misrepresentation of the father on the son, for we read in the 26th chapter of Genesis that his son, Isaac, got into a hard place, and he said of his little wife, Rebecca, "She is my sister." There the mantle of the father had fallen on the son, but, beloved, "chickens come home to roost," for we read now, in the 27th chapter of Genesis that when Isaac was old and almost blind, that his son, Jacob, covered himself with a goatskin and put on his brother Esau's clothes, and came in before the old Father Isaac, and behold he said, "I am your very son Esau." There is the sin handed down from the father to the son, and to the grandson. How strange that Jacob would cover himself with a goatskin in order to deceive his dying father! But God is faithful and will reward each man according to his deeds.

After Jacob deceived his father by putting on a goatskin and Esau's clothes, he swindled his brother Esau out of his birthright and his father's parting blessing. But we then read that Jacob left home and fled from the face of his brother Esau, and went into a far country and hired himself out to a man whose name was Laban, and Laban was a relative of Jacob's grandfather Abraham, and now we see Laban comes into play at this time, and takes a hand in deception. Jacob had fallen desperately in love with Laban's first [*sic*.] daughter, Miss Rachel, and he was so in love with this beautiful maiden that he finally contracted to work for her seven years, and when the seven years were up and the great wedding day was set, behold Laban covers Miss Leah with a heavy veil and presents her to Jacob for his daughter Rachel, and after the wedding ceremonies were all over, and Jacob was rejoicing in the fact that his seven years were up, and now he had his beautiful bride, Miss Rachel, behold to his surprise, when the veil was removed, he found that Laban had deceived him, and had given him Leah. Then no doubt his mind turned back to the day seven years before when he himself had put on a goatskin and deceived his old father, and had gotten Esau's blessing and birthright.

We see again, that the seed of deception is still bearing fruit in the family of Abraham, for as he had deceived his father, now Laban had deceived him. But Jacob was desperately in love with Rachel, and signed another contract to work seven years longer for Rachel. Finally he succeeded and won the girl that he had worked for fourteen years. But we also read again in the 31st chapter of Genesis that during this period of time Laban deceived Jacob not only in giving him Leah when he should have had Rachel, but that he changed his wages ten times. Also we read at this time that little Rachel comes to the front and takes a hand in the deception and stole one of her father's household gods and covered this god with household goods, and deceived the old man, and made him believe that she didn't have it.

But the end is not yet, for we read again in the 37th chapter of Genesis, that Jacob's ten oldest sons were in the field, keeping their father's flocks, and little Joseph and Benjamin were at home with their father, and Jacob sends Joseph out to the field to see how his ten sons were getting along, and Joseph's brethren caught the lad Joseph, and stripped him of the beautiful coat his father had made him, and killed a young goat and dipped Joseph's coat in the blood, and brought it to the father and said, "See if you can tell whether or not this is your son Joseph's coat." And Jacob said, "Yes, this is my son's coat, and no doubt an evil beast has torn him to pieces." But while they were carrying the coat to their father, little Joseph, whom they had just sold to a company of Ishmaelites that were going into Egypt, was at that time on his way to Egypt. What a wonderful case of deception! Jacob killed a goat and put on its hide and deceived his father, and now his sons kill a goat and roll Joseph's beautiful coat in its blood, and deceive their father, and we see again, that the seed of deception that was sown in the great-grand-father of these young men is still bearing fruit.

But the end is not yet, for many years later we read in the 42d chapter of Genesis that these same ten brethren that sold Joseph and dipped his coat in blood and deceived their father, are now standing in the presence of the governor of Egypt. They didn't know that it was their little brother Joseph, and he treated them as spies, and had them put in prison. While they were in prison they talked between themselves, and said, "No doubt, but this is our sin, that has over-taken us, for the way we treated our little brother Joseph." And Joseph heard their conversation and it almost broke his heart, and he had to flee from their presence and go out where he could weep.

How strange this story all ends. Joseph is a type of Christ; his brothers represent a perishing world coming to Christ, seeking the bread of life. It also brings out the two works of grace, for when they went to Egypt the first time, they saw Joseph as a great ruler, but they got their sacks full of corn; but when they went to Egypt the second time they knew Joseph then as their brother, and they got several wagon loads of corn, and honey, and the good things of the land. So it is with the young convert. He sees Jesus Christ as the ruler of the world, but when he is sanctified wholly he sees Jesus as his Elder Brother.

The Deceitfulness of Pride

The reader will remember that the wise man said that "Pride goeth before destruction and a haughty spirit before a fall." We have no-ticed that when a man gets on a tailor-made suit of clothes that is supposed to be all-wool, he begins to puff, and strut, and swagger, and grin, and smile, and any man could see at a glance that the man is laboring under a delusion. He thinks he is wearing new clothes, and he is too dull to know that he is wearing secondhand goods. He tells you that his suit is all-wool, and tailor-made, and he doesn't seem to remember that the old wether wore that wool all last year, and never thought of taking the "swell-head" once. But the gentleman threw that old sheep on the scaffold and sheared the wool off of his back and made himself a suit of clothes, and today he has a bad case of the "swell-head" because his clothes are all wool. Shame on a man that will take the wool off of a sheep's back and put it on his own back, and take a bad case of the "swaggers," and seems to forget that his clothes are secondhand.

Again we have noticed some man with a pair of shop made shoes on, and as he strutted, and showed off, and swaggered around you, he was showing you his shop made shoes. It seemed too that he had forgotten that he was wearing secondhand goods, for evidently he had forgotten that the old Jersey cow had worn that hide for the last seven or eight years, and never for a single time showed the spirit of pride, but this man knocked her in the head and pulled her hide off and tanned it, and made himself a pair of shoes to cover up the bunions and corns on his toes, and now because his bare feet are covered with a cowhide he has got a bad case of the "swaggers," and as truly as "staggers" will kill a mule, the "swaggers" will kill a man. "Blind staggers" are no more fatal to a mule than "blind swaggers" are to a man.

Again I have noticed ladies with an ostrich plume in their hat, and they wanted the eyes of the community to behold their beauty and grandeur and glory, and as they have stood before the mirror and beheld themselves, they seemed to think they had produced the feather, and behold, an old ostrich wore that feather all last year and never seemed to become proud or vain or to think that he himself was anything out of the ordinary. For an ostrich has got less sense than anything in the world, unless it is another creature that is trying to play the ostrich.

At other times we have seen a woman come into church with a silk dress on, and as she went down the aisle she wiggled and twisted exactly like a worm. She seemed to forget that the silkworm had been dressed in the silk before it ever reached her, but strange as it seems to think of, this woman has the appearance of a worm as she wiggles. No doubt her object is to show that she is wearing imported goods, but she forgets that the goods are, nevertheless, secondhand, and the human family seem to forget that the sheep wore the wool before the man, and the cow wore the hide before we got it, and the ostrich wore the plume before the woman put it on her head, and that the little worms made the silk before the woman ever wiggled down the aisle, cutting all the capers of a little innocent worm.

The reader will remember that when her pastor called on her to pray that morning, in her prayers in a choked, smothered voice, she told the Lord that she was a poor weak worm of the dust, but a few minutes ago she was trying to play the silkworm, all of which reveals the pride that is hid away in the heart of an unsanctified soul. Beloved, the wise man was right when he refers to pride as one of the great dangers of the human family, for it has often been said that "Pride is not a misfortune, but a disease."

9

A Few Things that Prove Depravity

IN THE SEVENTH CHAPTER of Romans, St. Paul says, "I am carnal, sold under sin." The apostle means to say that he was on the bottom and sin was on top, or in other words, the enemy had him down, and the thing that he said had him down was carnality. However, many of the big preachers tell us that, when man fell, he fell up instead of down, and that for six thousand years man has been pressing toward the "golden age." They have denied inbred sin and carnality, and declared publicly that these things were all believed only by the ignorant and weak-minded.

But we see a big difference between the teachings of the preachers and the presidents of the national banks of America. For the presidents of the national banks are spending millions of dollars in building vaults to keep their wealth in. They believe that man is depraved, and to make it right plain, they deal with every man as though he was a rascal. And no banker will trust his money in the hands of a man without he has good security. If a stranger was to go to a banker, and tell the banker that he was born as an angel and knew nothing of depravity and carnality, and that he wanted to borrow a few thousand dollars on his own face, the president of the bank would notify the health officers that there was an insane man in the bank, to come over and take him out. But, when we think of it, everything we see as we travel the streets proves that man fell down instead of up. For we see great signs that say, "Don't spit on the sidewalk," "Don't pull the flowers," "Don't feed the animals," "Don't bother the monkeys," "Keep off the grass," "Not responsible for hats and overcoats," "Keep out of the president's room," "Trespassers will be prosecuted." All of this shows that man has lost confidence in man.

10

The Five Things Necessary to Get You to Heaven

THERE ARE FIVE THINGS that a man must believe and be in possession of to get into heaven. You will understand that there are many things that he may have and might be able to use for his own good and for the glory of God, but there are only five things according to the old Book that are essential.

First, we must accept of the atonement, for we read in Hebrews 9th chapter 22d verse, "Without shedding of blood, there is no remission," so we see in this text that we must accept the atonement in order to get rid of sin.

Second, we read in Luke 13 chapter 3d verse the words of Jesus, "Except ye repent, ye shall all likewise perish." So we see in this text that it is necessary to repent in order to get to heaven. And St. Paul tells us in 2 Corinthians 7th chapter 8th to 10th verse, that repentance is a godly sorrow for sin. Now you will notice that these two things are essential, the atonement and repentance.

Third, we read in Hebrews 11th chapter 6th verse, the words of the great apostle as he says, "Without faith it is impossible to please God. For he that cometh to God must believe that he is, and that he is a rewarder of them that diligently seek him." We see faith is one of the essentials in order to get to heaven.

Fourth, we read in St. John 3d chapter 3d verse. the words of Jesus, "Verily, verily, I say unto thee, except a man be born again, he cannot see the kingdom of God." So we see the new birth is one of the essentials, as we go up the scale toward heaven.

Fifth, in Hebrews 12th chapter 14th verse, the apostle tells us that we must "Follow peace with all men, and holiness without which no man shall see the Lord."

So these are the five essentials—the atonement, repentance, faith, the new birth, and holiness. These are the five things that you must have. Amen! I am in possession of them right now.

11

The Marks of the Loss of First Love

In REVELATION 2:4 CHRIST SAID to a certain church, "I have somewhat against thee, because thou hast left thy first love." The reader will notice that Christ doesn't say that you have lost your first love, but He says you have left your first love. I used to think that it meant that we had lost the first love that came into our hearts when we were converted. But I don't think that is what He means at all. I think He means to teach here that this church had let their beautiful building, maybe their pipe organ, and hardwood pews, and Brussells carpets, and their well organized choir, their splendid official board, and all the machinery of the church have the first place in their affections, and Jesus had to take the second place. Therefore, they had left their first love, and this proves to me that Jesus must have the first place or He will not be satisfied, and no thinking man would expect Him to be. Now, for a little while, let's you and I study together some of the marks of the loss of first love.

First, when Jesus hasn't got the first place, we get into religious bondage, and our religious work has the first place in our affections, and we get under bondage in serving the church instead of the Lord.

Second, when Jesus hasn't got the first place, we have no religious joy, and we become dry, and juiceless and toothless and powerless and dead, though we may be very active in church activities.

Third, when Jesus hasn't got the first place, we become critical, and it is so easy then to criticize everybody in the world, for if Christ is not on the throne, we will get on the throne, and then we are ready to criticize everybody that doesn't measure up to our ideal.

Fourth, when Christ hasn't the first place, there is a lack of secret prayer, and a prayerless life is a helpless life. And not only helpless but powerless. And we must prevail with the Lord in secret prayer or we will not prevail at all. And there is nothing more dangerous to the life than to neglect secret prayer.

Fifth, when Jesus hasn't first place in our affections, we have no love for precious immortal souls, though we are busy in church work, and very active looking after the temple. It is not the love of souls that causes us to attend church, but it is more for the love of our own work and our institution, which is right within itself if it only bore the proper relations to Christ.

Sixth, when Christ hasn't first place in our affections, we lose interest in the study of our Bibles, and the Bible becomes a dead letter to us, and many hours we spend with the daily papers that would have been spent with our Bibles if Jesus had the first place.

Seventh, when Jesus hasn't first place in our affections, we find it very easy to stay away from prayer-meetings, and to give the hours to worldly pleasures, and in looking after the affairs of this life. And we often make excuses for not going to the house of the Lord, when really the only excuse is that Jesus has lost His first place in our affections, and other things have the first place, and Jesus has the second place.

Eighth, when Jesus hasn't the first place in our affections, we will lose interest in the doctrine and experience of entire sanctification, and we look on it as a kind of a luxury that we can accept or reject according to our own will or wish, and we become blind to the fact that sanctification is not a mere dessert that can be taken or let alone, after your meals, but it is the dinner itself. And if you neglect it, the knickknack will be of no profit in the world to you. For a laboring man needs a dinner, and not a nickel's worth of ice cream.

Ninth, when Christ hasn't the first place in our affections, we will be more or less under the dominion of the man-fearing spirit, and we will become cowardly, and we will be afraid to stand for the truth for fear of popular opinion, and we will be afraid to meet the frowns and the criticisms of the world and a backslidden church around and about us. And because of these things, when we are called on to pray, we will beg to be excused. And when we are called on to testify, we will get up in an embarrassed manner and notify the speaker that we never speak in public, when at the same time on worldly matters we can talk two ways at once. All of this is because Jesus has lost the first place in our affections.

Tenth, when Jesus has lost the first place in our heart, there will be a lack of watchfulness on our part, and we are at least liable to become too familiar with this old world. And we and the world will become so familiar that the world will rob us of what gold we have, and leave us nothing but a little brass.

Eleventh, when Jesus has lost the first place in our affections, we become stingy and tight-fisted with our money that we ought to give the Lord, and we rob God of His tenth and then rob Him of His offerings. Then we make ourselves believe that we have given all we are able to give.

Twelfth, when Jesus has lost the first place in our hearts, there will be a craving for worldly pleasures, and worldly amusements. It will be easy to hang around the shows and circuses, and theaters, and frolics. All because Christ hasn't the first place.

Thirteenth, when Christ has lost the first place in our affections, we have no insight into the Word of God, and the Book becomes sealed, and its treasures are hidden, and if we try to quote Scripture, we will become bunglers of the Word and not teachers of the Word.

12

Set Thy House in Order, for Thou Shalt Die

In 2 Kings twentieth chapter first verse we have this declaration through the Lord, "Set thine house in order; for thou shalt die, and not live." We want to notice why a man should set his house in order.

First, because we read in Hebrews ninth chapter seventh verse, "And as it is appointed unto men once to die, but after this the judgment." As man is judgment day bound, therefore he should set his house in order.

Second, he should set his house in order because of the uncertainty of life. Life is uncertain and death is sure, and death is on the track of every man, and the world in which we live is a dangerous world. There are ten thousand dangers on every side of man as he travels along the journey from this world to heaven. In fact, death is so certain that there has never been but two men gotten out of this world alive, and they were both holiness men—Enoch and Elijah.

Third, we should set our houses in order because of the certainty of death. As truly as we are here today, we shall go there tomorrow. No way of escape; the death angel is ready.

Fourth, we must set our houses in order, because if we do not do it, it will bring sorrow to us and our loved ones forever. For the hardest job in the world for a preacher to do is to preach the funeral of a man when he has no evidences of his reaching heaven.

Fifth, we must set our houses in order because we must meet God and give an account of our stewardship here below. And every man feels that he owes a debt to the Lord that he sooner or later must settle.

Sixth, we must set our houses in order here, for this is the only world in which it can be done. The crowd of backslidden preachers that are running up and down the land disputing God's Word to His face and offering the ungodly a second probation in the next world are themselves the dupes of the Devil, for the Bible nowhere offers men a chance of repentance beyond the grave. And as we have just given you a few reasons why you should set your house in order, we will now give you a few scriptures showing you how it can be done.

In John, 16th chapter 7th and 8th verses, we have Bible conviction, Christ said, "When the Holy Ghost is come, he will reprove the world of sin, and of righteousness, and of judgment."

In the second place, in Luke 13 chapter 3d verse Christ said, "Except ye repent, ye shall all likewise perish." And in 2 Corinthians 7th chapter 9th and 10th verses, St. Paul said, "Repentance is a godly sorrow for sin that needeth not to be repented of." He means to teach there that the sinner is sorry that he did the thing and is not merely sorry that he got caught at it. All rascals are sorry that they are caught but few of them are sorry that they did the thing.

Third, we must confess our sins in order to get rid of them. We read in 1 John 1st chapter 9th verse, "If we confess our sins, he is faithful and just to forgive us our sins."

Fourth, we must forsake our sins. In Proverbs 28th chapter 13th verse King Solomon said, "Whoso covereth his sins shall not prosper, but whoso confesseth and forsaketh them shall have mercy." Here we notice that to confess sin is not as much as God requires. His requirements are confess and forsake. The most of sinners confess their sins every day, but while they do so they hold on to their sins with a death grip until, like the sinners of old, they hold on to them till they damn them.

Fifth, we must believe on the Lord Jesus Christ. In Acts 16th chapter 31st verse, St. Paul says, "Believe on the Lord Jesus Christ, and thou shalt be saved, and thine house." Here St. Paul seems to teach a household religion, for he declared if this man would believe on the Lord Jesus Christ that there was at least a possibility of the whole family finding God.

Sixth, we must be justified by faith, and St. Paul said in Romans 5th chapter 1st verse, "Therefore being justified by faith, we have peace with God through our Lord Jesus Christ." Here the theologian tells us that justification means a legal act and really takes place in the mind of God.

Seventh, we must be regenerated. In Paul's letter to Titus the 3rd chapter and 5th and 6th verses, Paul said, "Not by works of righteousness which we have done, but according to his mercy he saved us by the washing of regeneration and renewing of the Holy Ghost, which he shed on us abundantly." Here the reader will notice the distinction between justification and regeneration. While justification takes place in the mind of God, regeneration takes place in the heart of man, and those who are in authority and position to know, tell us that regeneration means to give life to those who once had it but lost it, and find that man lost his spiritual life in the fall, but he has been redeemed by Christ and bought back, and now God restores to him the beautiful spiritual life that he lost and, thank God, he may not and need not ever die again.

Eighth, we must receive the witness of the Spirit, and we read in Romans 8th chapter 16th verse,, "The Spirit itself beareth witness with our spirit that we are the children of God. And if children, then heirs; heirs of God, and joint heirs with Christ." Now here we find that the witness of the Spirit is even different from justification and regeneration. While justification takes place in the mind of God, regeneration is in the heart of man. Here our heavenly Father in His goodness and mercy sends the Holy Spirit into our heart and life and gives us a conscious knowledge of the fact that our sins have been blotted out, and we have the blessed assurance now of our home in heaven.

Ninth, we must be adopted into the family of God. We read in 1 John 3d chapter, and the first three verses, "Behold, what manner of love the Father hath bestowed upon us that we should be called the sons of God. Therefore the world knoweth us not, because it knew him not. Beloved, now are we the sons of God, and it doth not yet appear what we shall be, but we know that when he shall appear, we shall be like him, for we shall see him as he is, and every man that hath this hope in him purifieth himself, even as he is pure." Here the reader will notice that it means so very much to be adopted into the royal family, and this makes Romans 8th chapter 16th verse very plain, where Christ declares that we become "heirs of God, and joint heirs with Christ." We see here that an heir is much more than a mere servant, for we belong to the family and have all the rights of lawful heirs. Amen, for our wonderful and glorious possession!

13

The Tree that is Dead at the Top

HOW STRANGE SOME THINGS strike you that you have been accustomed to all your life, and yet under some conditions the thing will strike you in a new place, and you will be surprised and will wonder that you never saw the thing that you have probably seen all your life. To illustrate: One morning while walking through an apple orchard in the beautiful Boise valley in southern Idaho, I walked up to a large apple tree and behold at the top of it was dead, and ready to tumble down, but the lower limbs were alive and hanging full of beautiful Roman Beauties. And it struck me with such force that I stood and looked on with wonder and amazement. Of course I have seen many trees that were dead at the top, while there was life in the lower limbs, but on this occasion I stood bewildered and wondered at what I beheld. Here was one part of the tree dead and lifeless, and the other part alive and bearing fruit. The lower limbs were so full of the beautiful apples that they seemed to hang nearly to the ground, and no life or fruit at the top of the tree.

Well, I said to myself, "Here before me stands the American church, just as I have seen it in my travels. The great leaders of the church, who are the top of the institution, are not soul winners. They have gone out of the soul-saving business; many of them don't believe in conversion any more. They have not made an altar call in many years. They are too important to get down at a mourner's bench with a penitent sinner and help pray him through, and in that case they are like the apple tree. The thing is dead at the top. While many more of the great leaders of our leading denominations are woefully tainted with higher criticism, and worse still even with destructive criticism, and they are wonderfully mixed up with Unitarianism, and have stubbornly rejected the atoning blood of a crucified Savior. Others are tainted with Universalism, while sadder still, many others seem to have a warm side for Christian Science, and strange to say, even Russellism has found a place in the top of this tree. While we must admit that the only life-saving crew in the church are the lower order of the ministers, or the laity, which the reader will see are the lower limbs on this tree." But then another thought came into my mind that made me sad. It was this: I said, "Now, if the top of the tree is dead, is the fruit on the lower limbs as sound, and as nutritious as it would be if the top of the tree was full of life?" Then I wondered if the decay from the dying top would eventually work down the tree until it would finally destroy the life that was in the lower limbs, and in my mind I saw it going on. I saw the tree die below the lower limbs, and behold there stood before me a dead tree and no fruit on it at all. Yet there the tree was occupying the same ground it had occupied when alive and full of fruit.

I began to wonder: I said, "How long will a man have to irrigate that tree and fertilize that soil to put life back into that tree?" And at that time I remembered hearing a young man say, who was full of life and fire, that "We are going to swing our church back to holiness, we are going to bring her back to life. We are laying plans now to irrigate that dead tree and fertilize her and prune her and spray her, and put her to bearing fruit again." And yet I have looked on with wonder, and the more the soil was cultivated and the better it was fertilized, the deader that tree became, until finally the lower limbs themselves had dropped off one at a time, and there stood before me a large trunk of a dead tree, and behold the birds came and built their nests under the bark and in its rotten wood, and the bugs and lizards and even the screech owls got into that rotten tree and made it their nest. And in my mind I saw the large serpent coiled there, and I said, "How strange, that used to be a fruit-bearing tree. But behold, death and decay got into the top of it and was allowed to remain until it destroyed the whole tree." A week later a layman in the church said to me, "I don't accept the doctrine and experience of holiness because our leaders reject it." And I said, "There is the tree that I saw in my vision. Death struck her in the top and was working toward the ground, and surely and truly as the tree died at the top, it will not be a generation until every limb on that tree is dead and dropping off."

We might wind up by saying that unbelief in the pulpit will put unbelief in the pew, and worldliness in the pulpit will put formalism in the pew; and if you discover a polar bear in the pulpit, you may look for icebergs in the pew. The polar bear must have ice. And how many times have I seen a church that was warm and on fire for God, receive a learned doctor in their pulpit, and he was as spiritually dead as the tree was literally dead, and it wouldn't be twelve months until he had cooled off and choked out and starved out the spiritual life of his entire flock, and now they are as dead and as worldly as he himself. This is one of the kind of the twentieth century. Think of it, here is a congregation paying their preacher their hard-earned money to help them to live right, and get to heaven, and behold, he is undermining their faith in the deity of Jesus, and the inspiration of the Scriptures, and he will finally rob them of their living faith, and rob them of heaven and populate hell with them. Now, let the reader look back and see if he can see anything in that tree that resembles the American church. And beloved reader, if you have any spiritual life, this picture that we have just shown you will just about scare you to death. And, beloved, you had better rise up in your God-given power, and by the grace of God, and the blood of Jesus Christ, and the power of the Holy Ghost, shake off all doubt and fear and flee to the outstretched arms of a loving, gentle, tender, sympathizing Jesus, "Who loved you and gave himself for you that he might redeem you from all iniquity and purify unto himself a peculiar people, zealous of good works."

14

The River Jordan

I HAVE JUST BEEN reading and thinking and studying about the River Jordan. Some things in the last few years have become so interesting to me, and one of the interesting things to me is this wonderful river that we call Jordan. There is no river in the world that has been talked of so much, and so many beautiful things spoken and written about as have been said and written about this remarkable river.

It was the River Jordan that God drew a line through and cut off the waters from the waters and opened the way by which the Israelites might pass through from the wilderness into the land of Canaan. The reader will remember that we have already written of the passage of the Israelites through this remarkable river, and they piled up twelve stones in the bottom of the River Jordan, and also took up twelve stones and laid them on their shoulders and carried them out from the bottom of this river, and laid them on the banks of Jordan for their public testimony. It was the River Jordan that Elijah smote with his overcoat, and the waters parted before him. It was the River Jordan also that the young Elisha smote with the same overcoat and said, "Where is the God of Elijah?" It was in the River Jordan that later on in life Elisha made the iron to swim. It was in the River Jordan that Naaman dipped seven times, and was cured of leprosy, and his flesh became as the flesh of a child. And behold it was in the River Jordan that John the Baptist baptized the Lord Jesus Christ, when the blessed Holy Ghost descended as a beautiful white dove, and abode upon Him. Evidently He was in the river, or nearby when this wonderful transaction took place.

Some of the most wonderful events in sacred history occurred in connection with the River Jordan. We see that the River Jordan has been a place for the last century where the tourists, pilgrims, and travelers have gone to look upon those wonderful waters, until today the River Jordan is one of the most interesting streams in the world to a New Testament Christian. We notice that this river has its source back in a beautiful mountain range, and makes it way down through the beautiful Jordan valley, and the stream is fed from the melted snows of Lebanon, and the bubbling springs along the Jordan valley.

It was in this valley where Abraham, Isaac, and Jacob used to water their flocks. It was this beautiful Jordan valley that attracted the eye of the young man Lot, when he broke with his uncle Abraham and pitched his tent toward Sodom. We read that he lifted up his eyes and beheld the Jordan valley. His prospects for a business man were very bright then. He had a fine start, but what a sad ending! But as interesting as this river is, there is something very sad about the River Jordan. After all that we have seen and heard that was beautiful, we now have to behold the River Jordan winding down through those lovely valleys and finally plunging over into the Dead Sea, and the Dead Sea opens her mouth and swallows the River Jordan, and behold this beautiful river of sparkling waters, full of life, becomes as dead as the Dead Sea. And though the River Jordan has been emptying itself into the Dead Sea for thousands of years, yet she has never been able to reform the Dead Sea. The sea is so dead now that no life can exist in it, and strange to say, the River Jordan is still emptying itself into this sea of death, and the Dead Sea is as dead now as she was two thousand years ago.

As I have studied this question I said again, "There is another picture of the American church. For the last fifty years, since the days of Dr. and Mrs. Phoebe Palmer, the great holiness move, which is full of life and juice and fire, and unction and glory, has been fed by the sparkling waters from the river of life, with hundreds of thousands saved and sanctified at her altars, this wonderful revival has emptied herself into the American church, just as the River Jordan empties itself into the Dead Sea. Though hundreds of thousands from the holiness movement have gone into the American church, the leaders themselves confess that the church is deader now than she was twenty-five years ago; and, beloved, if that is the case, don't you see some marks of similarity between the River Jordan and the Dead

Sea, and the holiness movement and the American church? Then we are made to wonder, is there any hope, will the River Jordan ever reform the Dead Sea, will she ever bring her back to life? We must answer no; for although this beautiful river has flowed into this sea for thousands of years, there are still no signs of life. And while the holiness movement is still turning annually a flood of life and glory into the American church, Dead Sea like she opens her mouth and swallows them and they die just as dead as the rest of the institution.

Then we stop and ask again, is there any hope? We will say, "Yes, when we look in another direction." It is this, for all hands to go to work and cut a new channel for the River Jordan, and turn her course down some other beautiful valley, and let this sparkling, fresh water, flow out over the great valleys of that land, and irrigate the good soil that is lying dead, and then you will see life and not death. And now, the hope of the holiness movement is that the channels shall be cut, and that she may be turned into a new valley, that she may irrigate these great fields in America and bring forth fruit to the glory of God and the good of humanity. For we see as long as the River Jordan empties into the Dead Sea, there is no hope of life, and as long as the holiness movement empties itself into this great dead ecclesiastical body, it will just open its mouth, Dead Sea like, and swallow up everything that has life, and the thing it swallows will die just as dead as the thing that swallowed it. And this all proves to me that there is great need of a new move in this land, that God's holy people may unite in a great progressive body to irrigate and fertilize and cultivate and spray and prune the great orchards that God is expecting us to plant out and cultivate. It can be done, and it ought to be done, and if we don't do it, we will be the eternal losers, in this world and in the world to come. And I am ready to say with Joshua of old, "As for me and my house, we will serve the Lord."

But what if you should hear the River Jordan say, "Oh, no, let's not quit the old ship, let us flow on into the Dead Sea; by and by we are going to reform the Dead Sea, and some day we will sit down on the banks of the Dead Sea and it will be working alive with the beautiful black bass and rainbow trout and speckled perch, and the buffalo, and spotted rock." Now who believes that the Dead Sea will ever turn out such material as that?

There is a picture that I have had hanging on the walls of my memory for several years. I want you to read it, and then sit down and think it over and see what God says to you, and see if you don't think you had better throw your life and energy into the cutting of that new channel and trying to save the River Jordan from the hands of the Dead Sea. And I will meet you at the marriage supper of the Lamb, washed and robed, and ready for the feast. Amen!

15

This Great Salvation

IN THE 2ND CHAPTER of Hebrews and third verse, we have one of the greatest questions that God ever asked man. The question is enough to scare a man to death. It is the unanswerable question. God says, "How shall we escape if we neglect so great salvation?" Just why the Lord asked man a question he couldn't answer, is a mystery, but still He did it. I suppose that neither our heavenly Father, nor man, can answer the question. For if a man neglects the salvation of his soul, there is no escape, for we read in Hebrews 9:27, "And as it is appointed unto men once to die, so after this the judgment." Therefore, we are all headed toward that great day and we will have to go and stand before the King, and it may be possible that we will find out that through the goodness of our heavenly Father, He asks us this question in order to wake us up, and to alarm and arouse our dead, slumbering conscience, that we might arise and bestir ourselves, and if possible make the escape from an eternal doom. But as we see there is no escape and we can't answer the question, thank the Lord there is still hope, for we can talk about the greatness of our salvation.

First, salvation is great because God himself is the author of it, and everything God does is great. His little things are some of His greatest things. In the days of King Solomon they used the little red ants for their college presidents. And when Solomon met a lazy, trifling, good for nothing fellow he sent him off to college, and when he got there he met a red ant, and Solomon said, "Learn wisdom." Again Solomon said, "The spider taketh hold with her hands, and is in kings' palaces." The ant represents works, and the spider represents faith. Solomon said, "The ant layeth up her store in the harvest time, and the spider is in kings' palaces." To show you that the ant had more sense than lots of men, in Jeremiah 8th chapter 20th verse, Jeremiah said, "The harvest is past, the summer is ended, and we are not saved." So if the ant had sense enough to lay up his store in harvest time, and man fails to do it, then the ant is more sensible than man. And the spider had taken hold with her little hands, and had gotten into the king's palace, and everybody wants to get into the palace of the king. The spider, being a representative of faith, takes hold with her hand and spins her web out of that which is invisible. No man can see with his physical eye the material that the spider uses in making her beautiful gown.

And so faith is invisible, but by faith we take hold with our hands, and spiderlike, we finally weave us beautiful garments, the most beautiful things the human eye ever beheld, as they are woven by that which is invisible. Now again the old Book says that our life is like the flying of the shuttle. There are two things about a shuttle, the first is it goes with great speed, but the most beautiful thing about it is, it pulls the thread as it travels along, and the threads are various colors. When we have trouble the shuttle pulls a black thread; when we have happiness it pulls a beautiful red thread, and when we have joy it pulls a white thread, and when we are overflowing with love it pulls a beautiful blue thread. And when the garment has been woven behold we have all colors in it, and it takes these colors all mingled together to make the beautiful garment. If it was all trouble the garment would be of only one color, or if it was all happiness it would only be of one color, but all of these, the different trials and blessings mingled together, will make up the beautiful robe of righteousness that we are to weave with the hand of faith. And we will understand what Solomon meant when he said, "The spider taketh hold with her hands, and is in kings' palaces." So we see that God's least things are some of His greatest things, and they teach us some of the most beautiful lessons as we journey from earth to heaven.

Salvation is Great Because it is Both a Secret and a Mystery

In the 25th Psalm and 12th verse we read "the secret of the Lord is with them that fear him, and he will show them his covenant." We next notice in the 3d chapter of Ephesians that St. Paul said that "Salvation is a mystery that hath been hid from the ages, but is now revealed by the Lord Jesus Christ." Now there is something peculiar and strange concerning secrets and a mystery. As strange as it is, they have always had a wonderful fascination to the human family. The average man or woman is loaded down with secrets. Men sit up at night and watch their secrets. Women have worn the soles off of their shoes trotting over town looking for a secret. Some men have rode the goat all night in search of a secret, and some women have looked for and trotted after the Eastern Star in the hope that they might hear or find out some secret. We find that salvation is both a secret and a mystery united, and we found that secret and a mystery are not exactly the same. Yet they are so closely related .that you can scarcely tell where one ends and the other begins. I can give you a plain, practical, common sense illustration:

Along about the first night in the month of April a man goes out into his garden and plants an Irish potato. Nobody saw him plant it there, that was a secret. But two weeks later the potato comes up and the secret gets out. Two months later he goes to this potato hill and will scratch out a washpan full of Irish potatoes. This one little potato multiplied itself into one dozen big potatoes. Now there is the mystery connected with the secret. But you say, "How can you apply this to a Christian experience?" Well, we will do this:

We will say that away back under the dispensation of the Father the plan was laid and the potato was planted, and when Jesus was born in Bethlehem of Judea, the potato came up, and the secret got out, as they generally do, and on the day of Pentecost, when there were three thousand converted, that was "potato-digging" day. There was the secret and the mystery united, and worked out so plain that if a man can get one idea through his noggin, he can understand both a secret and a mystery.

The Cost of this Great Salvation

Another reason why salvation is the greatest thing in the world is because it cost more than anything else in the world. It is the only thing that ever cost much. But salvation cost God His Son, and Jesus Christ every drop of His blood, and thirty-three years absence from His home, and it cost heaven its brightest Jewel. The beautiful city of God was without the Christ for thirty-three years. We can't imagine what heaven would be without Jesus, and yet the home of God had no Son in it for thirty-three long years. During that time the Son of God walked the Judean hills and worked at the carpenter's trade to make His bread. He preached on the streets of the cities and slept on the mountainside at night. He did all this for a lost, perishing, doomed, hopeless world. Bless His name! He was in search of fallen humanity. Man had fallen and had lost his holy estate and the Son of God was in search of him, and thank God, He found him, and the beautiful story of the shepherd in search of his sheep is nothing more nor less than the Son of God looking for me. Don't let us forget that the Devil had the human family on the auctioneer's block and was bidding us off and buying us in for the express purpose of damning us forever.

Thank God, Jesus appeared on the scene just in time to put in the highest bid and purchase a diamond in the rough, and bring home the lost sheep. It has been said that He bought man with the gold of His blood, and the silver of His tears; therefore, the redemption of man is the costliest thing in the world. We have often heard people say that everything costs; that they had paid a hundred dollars for their cow, but God has said long ago, that "the gold is mine, and the cattle is mine," therefore the cow really cost us nothing, for we paid for God's cow with God's money, but it is different when it comes to the price of your soul. For Jesus tasted death that we might taste of life: He became the Son of man that we might become the sons and daughters of the Almighty. Jesus left heaven and came into this world that He might open up a way by which we could get out of this world and go into heaven. He put on humanity that we might put on divinity. When He bore the Roman scourge it was for you and for me. He had looked down from the throne and seen men under the lash, but Jesus had never been whipped until He came to redeem us. He went under the lash and endured it in order that a way might be opened up by which man could get out of the life of sin and bondage into a life of freedom and happiness. Jesus had seen the human family without a home, but He was never without a home until He came to redeem us and then we hear those beautiful words, but oh, so sad, "The foxes have holes and the birds of the air have nests, but the Son of man hath not where to lay his head."

Dear reader, isn't that strange talk for a person to use when He himself had built the world that He was walking on? and yet it was true. For we read His own words that He had created all things, and by Him all things were created and that He upholdeth all things by the right hand of His power, and yet He took the place of a pauper. When He was born into this world it was so arranged that He should be born in a wagon yard or a livery stable, that He was to work at the carpenter's trade, and paid His taxes. He literally traveled through this world as a lonely wanderer, and when He hung on the cross He was even refused a drink of water, and instead of a cup of cool refreshing sparkling water, he received a cup of gall, and yet this was the King of the world. But the first crown He ever wore as a King was the crown of thorns. While the world was trying to disgrace Him and heap shame and contempt on Him, their very attitude toward Jesus, and His attitude toward them has won for Him a name that is above every other name. And today there is not an infidel club in the world, but has to put on its billheads when they announce their services, the birth of Jesus. I say, shame on an infidel club that denies Jesus Christ, and yet can't hold an infidel meeting and get out their announcements but what they put on every billhead the birth of the Son of God. Every note that is given in a bank, and every deed to a tract of land and every mortgage that a man gives on his ranch, or a team of mules would be worthless without the birth of Jesus Christ on it. And all of this makes me shout, bless God, when I think that Jesus Christ with all the derision that is heaped on Him is the most popular being that ever was in this world, and to think that this wonderful Savior is mine!

Salvation is Great Because it Offers a Remedy for Sin

Salvation is the only thing that is known to man that offers a remedy for sin. Man has tried many inventions, he has worked overtime to think out some plan that would put him on his feet and deliver him from an internal bondage and struggle that he has carried all of his life, but they have all failed. They have tried civil law, and civic righteousness, education, and charitable institutions, and so far all remedies that man has ever invented have utterly failed. Some men for a remedy have denied that there was any sin; others have denied the existence of eternal punishment, hoping by so doing to find a remedy. Others have sneered at the Devil and swore until they were black in the face that he was not in existence; others have declared that we have a universal salvation, that all men will be saved, both good and bad. Other men in their bewilderment and sad predicament have decided that only a special few, that they term the elect, will be saved; and they imagine that the elect will be saved, it matters not how mean they are, and that all the rest of the human family was long ago predestined to damnation and will be eternally lost, it matters not how good they are. But after all, this is no remedy for the curse of sin. So we see that all human inventions and manmade remedies are tee-total failures. We remember that King David said that his enemies had made them gods of their own; he said they had eyes and didn't see and had ears and didn't hear; he said they had throats and could not speak through them, and he said the sinners of his day were as bad off as the gods they had made. The reader will see that the self-made gods were only man's remedy to get rid of sin, and yet all have failed. In our day we have a wonderful hurrah going on about the Fatherhood of God and the brotherhood of man. Some preachers have even quit the pulpit and given up preaching Christ, and are going up and down the land lecturing on the Fatherhood of God and the brotherhood of man. Then others have decided that the only God there is, is the God that is in man, that man himself is a divine being and that he is able to handle the situation. But they have all gone down in defeat, and will go down, for there is but one remedy in all the wide world and that is the salvation offered to man through the atoning blood of Jesus Christ, which is the only remedy for sin.

Salvation means deliverance from sin, and salvation is a double gift and a double blessing, because sin is a double tragedy and God provided a double remedy. In the 51st Psalm, King David said, "Blot out my transgression," and in the second verse he said, "Cleanse me from my sin," and we find that God provided a double remedy for this double disease. That is, pardon for the guilty, and cleansing for the believer, and in order to provide a double remedy, necessarily the atonement had to be doubled, for we find in Romans 5th chapter 8th verse, "But God commendeth his love toward us in that while we were yet sinners, Christ died for us." Here the reader will see the atonement reaching down to the sinner. But in the next place we see the atonement reaching down to the Church, for in Eph. 5th chapter 25th and 26th verses, "Husbands love your wives, even as Christ also loved the church and gave himself for it, that he might sanctify and cleanse it with the washing of water by the word, that he might present it to himself, a glorious church not having spot or wrinkle, or any such thing, but that it should be holy and without blemish." Here the reader will see the atonement reaching the Church, and while the sinner needs pardon, the Church needs cleansing, and thank God, we have the remedy for both through the shed blood of the crucified Son of God, which is the only remedy for sin in the whole world. Bless God, we have the remedy! We have got the goods, and in spite of an unbelieving Church, and a wicked world, we are delivering the goods just the same. Bless God!

Salvation is Great Because of the Extent of It

When we think of the extent of salvation our minds well-nigh reel and stagger, for we must evidently think of the depth to which man has fallen, and then to the heights of glory to which God intends to lift him. First, we must see the new birth, and the idea of being born of the Spirit carries with it a wonderful mystery. How it is that one moment a man can be a guilty sinner, and far out in a world of sin, and the next moment a truly regenerated believer, and far up in the world of righteousness, and yet that takes place when a man is born of the Spirit. For St. Paul tells us in Col. 1st chapter 13th verse that the meaning of the new birth is to be a deliverance from the power of darkness and to be translated into the kingdom of God's dear Son. So there we see first that salvation means deliverance from the powers of darkness, and second, a translation out of that dark world into the kingdom of light, for in John 8th chapter 12th verse Christ said, "I am the light of the world, and he that followeth me shall not walk in darkness, but shall have the light of life." And the idea of the new birth is really something new in the world, while it looks to us like it is old because we have heard of it all of our lives, yet the new birth was never heard of in the world until Jesus was born.

When He introduced the subject to the great and learned Nicodemus, it was the most astonishing thing that ever entered the head of that wonderful Jewish teacher. I don't wonder that the doctor scratched his head and said, "How can these things be?" He had thought much of sin, but he didn't know how to get out of it, but how new it was when Jesus said, "Nicodemus, the way to get out of sin is to be born out of it." Nicodemus had thought that changing climates and changing localities and changing your surroundings and your environments was probably a good remedy, but all the changes he had made had had no effect in the world on his moral condition, and he never heard of a remedy until he met Jesus. Thank God, some of the rest of us have heard of that remedy, have accepted it, and have shouted ourselves hoarse over the fact that, bless God, we have got it now. So Jesus is the author of the new birth. And it was something new under heaven. But it is just as new today as it was then, and our nation is now drifting to the place where many are rejecting the new birth because it is inexplainable by the theological teachers of our universities.

Beloved, when it comes to an explanation of the new birth the president of a university has no advantage over the washwoman. And for all this I say, "Glory to God!" That wonderful question of Nicodemus, "How can these things be?" is still ringing down over the hills of Judea, but it has reached down over the plains of earth, it has crossed the mighty deep. Beloved, an explanation of the new birth is not found under a plug hat, nor under the lapel of a double breasted broadcloth coat; thank God, it can be fully understood in the bosom of an uneducated man. One of the greatest mysteries connected with the salvation of a man's soul is seen in the fact that the unlearned knows as much about it as the cultured and brilliant.

I remember one morning when my heart was leaping for joy and bubbling over with the perfect love of God, a college president seemed to be insulted and with a look of defiance on his face, he said to me, "Sir, you are just a gosling and have not shed off your down yet, and and how dare you stand up and profess to be made perfect in love?"

I said, "Doctor, I have been saved for twelve years, and if the Son of God can't make a man perfect in love in twelve years, I defy you to prove that He can do it in twelve thousand." The doctor failed to make good, and I kept the blessing, thank God. But here is another little point that I don't want to forget while we are talking about the new birth. When Jesus said, "Ye must be born again," He absolutely left you without a choice. He didn't say you could take it or let it alone and get to heaven. He said, "Ye *must*," and beloved, if "ye *must*" then "ye must." And then He added this clause, "Without it ye can not see the kingdom of God." And when the learned turn up their noses and sneer, God never modifies it nor rounds off the corners, and has never taken it back from that hour till this. It stands out there in letters of fire, and reaches down to the gates of hell and up to the beautiful walls of the city above, and will stand out forever, and ever and ever, "Ye must be born again, or you can not see the kingdom of God."

I used to sing in the Salvation Army, "How well I remember in sorrow's dark night, how the lamp of His love shed its beautiful light. More grace He has given, and burdens removed, and over and over His goodness I've proved. And shall I turn back into the world, oh no, not I, not I, and shall I turn back into the world, oh no, not I." Many a dark drizzly night I have stood on the street corner and sung that song and beat the drum and called the wanderers to Jesus, and I have seen them kneel on the cold, muddy streets and in less than a minute I have seen them born of the Spirit and translated out of the kingdom of darkness into the kingdom of light, and have seen the tears plow a furrow down through their dirty faces. Thank God! Amen!

Salvation is Great because of the Fullness of the Blessing

Dear reader, we want you to see that a wonderful experience is promised to the sons and daughters of our heavenly Father in the 17th and 18th verses of the 5th chapter of Ephesians. Now listen to these wonderful words of the inspired apostle: "Wherefore be ye not unwise, but understanding what the will of the Lord is, and be not drunk with wine wherein is excess, but be filled with the Spirit." Here we have a direct command from the inspired apostle to be filled.

It doesn't mean half full, or three-quarters, but to be full. And we must remember, and we do remember, and then we don't propose to forget, that the most beautiful life in the world is a Spirit-filled life. No life is so beautiful as the Spirit-filled life. No life is so useful as the Spirit-filled life. In fact, the hope of your own soul and the hope of your family and the hope of your church of which you are a member, and the hope of the world in which you live, is only seen in this wonderful Spirit-filled life. No man is a success for God or himself that is not completely filled, led and controlled by the Holy Ghost. Without the Holy Ghost we would be failures. Without Him we would be helpless, indeed, without Him we would be hopeless. But, thank God, with Him difficulties are saddle horses, surrounding circumstances are stepladders, and impossibilities are springboards to leap off of and land right in the middle of a glorious victory. When the Holy Ghost comes, Christ said, "He will take the things of mine and show them to you." More than that, He said, "When he is come, he will bring all things to your remembrance whatsoever I have said unto you." He even went so far as to say, "For I will give you a mouth and a wisdom which all your adversaries will not be able to gainsay or resist." This refers, of course, to the incoming of the blessed Holy Ghost which is to do two things for you. First, He is to cleanse the temple, and second, He is to fill it. Then we might add a third clause and say that He is to rule it. For the Holy Ghost is today the executive of the Godhead in this world. And the men of the church that stubbornly reject Him have closed every avenue of victory and have shut the door of hope and success in their own face.

There is no institution in the world that is deader and more lifeless and hopeless than a church without the Holy Ghost. We can take the American church and we will see at a glance that she never had better buildings, their pews were never better made, their carpets are the best, their organs can not be improved on, they have a beautiful ritual, and, bless your heart, they know it. They can sing a verse and the pastor and the official board, their choir leader and all the congregation can say AH-MEN, and draw it out as long as your arm, and stand up so precisely, it looks like if they were to smile it would break their faces all to pieces, and they would ruin their religious service, and yet as beautiful as those things are, they are no more signs of life and juice and unction and glory, not a bit more than if there were no such things in existence. The machinery is good, but there is no oil on it. We might ask, What is the matter with this wonderful institution? No thinking man has to study for a minute to get the answer. They have just rejected the Holy Ghost, and they are running their institution without God. In many places we fear that He has taken His everlasting flight and He may never return. It is true that a church of this description will add members to its enrollment. They will send out cards beautifully printed, the very type itself is well set, the cards are gilt-edged, some will sign them up and drop them in the collection basket; others will come in by hitting the trail. Many others will come in on Decision day; and we are not abusing those methods; we are only stating that they can gather in members by those methods, but, beloved, does that look to you like an old-fashioned revival of heart-felt, Holy Ghost religion?

Sad to say that many of the people that come by those methods never go back to see how the institution is progressing. At a glance you can see they have no interest there because they have received nothing. But you let the pastor preach a series of sermons on the awfulness of sin and the horrors of hell and the glory of heaven, and eternal life until conviction seizes the hearts of men and they weep their way to a place of prayer, and are really born again and come into the Church of Jesus Christ by the gateway of the new birth, then her altars will be the most sacred place to them of any place in the world, and you can hardly keep them away from church. Then later on let the pastor preach a series of sermons on the Spirit-filled life, the power of the incoming of the Holy Ghost, the burning, surging glory of the sanctified experience, and the beauty of perfect love and such glorious themes until his entire church becomes so hungry for the fullness of the blessing until they will weep their way to a place of prayer, consecrate all, look up through their tears with simple faith and receive the Holy Ghost, and beloved, you will have a church that will march through this old world and the Devil will weep as the angels rejoice while the saints shout for joy. This church will be composed of a company of sky-openers and fire pullers, sin-killers, Devil-drivers, trench-diggers, water-haulers; and it takes all of the above to make a true soldier, and the Spirit-filled life will make you a soldier of the cross.

Bless God for the privilege of preaching this great salvation and seeing multiplied thousands pull till the skies open and dig till they strike water, and today they are feasting on the fat of the land, for they are living in the land of Canaan. You remember the beautiful song that we sing, that "It is good to live in Canaan where grapes of Eschol grow, it's good to live in Canaan where milk and honey flow." We will now act like the church where they all say *Ah-men*. For, glory to Jesus, the word "Amen," means, "Yes, Lord, and I'll pay my part."

16

Under His Wings

DEAR READER, FOR A few minutes let's you and I look at the 36th Psalm and 7th and 8th verses: "How excellent is thy lovingkindness O God; therefore the children of men put their trust under the shadow of thy wing. They shall be abundantly satisfied with the fatness of thy house and thou shalt make them drink of the rivers of thy pleasure." Here we have everything that we need to make us happy, as we journey through this world. First, we notice that we are to have God's love and kindness and in the second place that we are to abide in the shadow of God's wing. Just think how secure a man is if he is under the wings of the Almighty. There is not a devil in the pit or out of it that could get on the top of a building at night and throw a brickbat off on the man's head if he is under God's wing. That is the best protection that a man could have in the whole wide, wide world. Third, we notice that a man shall be abundantly satisfied with the fatness of God's house. Here we have the abundance of fat things which means spiritual food, spiritual protection, thank God! the abiding Comforter of the Holy Ghost. It means that God will touch our hearts and we will love right; He will touch our brain and we will think right; He will touch our eyes and we will see right; He will touch our ears and we will hear right.

All of that is included in a house of fat things. In the fourth place we notice that we are to drink out of a river of pleasure.

We know today that the world has gone pleasure-mad. There is no scheme that hell can concoct to entertain a lost world that the Devil hasn't pulled off during this generation, and sorry to say he has not only captured the world as we see them in their mad rush seeking pleasure, but he has actually invaded the house of God and has well-nigh captured both pulpit and pew. Series of lectures are put on now in the great churches sometimes running for two weeks on such subjects as "Government ownership," "Five cents' worth of beef liver," "One feather from the tail of the dog that flew at the tramp," "Will the future woman marry?" and such degrading subjects along now with the moving picture reels are taking the place of the preaching of the gospel of the Son of God.

When the church members can't find as much frolicking going on at the church as they desire, they even go to places that are very, very questionable, and there is a kind of a shadow that hangs over such places that would make a saint tremble in his soul to be found there, but cold, dead, formal church members are often seen around such questionable places. For six thousand years they have been on such searches for pleasure but will never overtake it, but will die on the trail, and many without God. But just think of it, God has said that His people will drink out of a river of pleasure. I judge that the real meaning of this statement is that God will give His people such quantities of satisfaction that He even compares it to a river. This is said by some to be satisfied satisfaction. For He has just said that we will be abundantly satisfied with the fatness of His house, and then He added, "and drinking out of a river of pleasure," which is without a doubt the best condition a soul could be in in this world.

17

A Wall of Fire

WELL, AMEN! WHILE READING in my Bible the other day I ran across this wonderful statement in 2nd chapter of Zechariah and the 5th verse: "I will be a wall of fire around about thee, and the glory in the midst thereof [*sic.*]." and I said, "Well, who in the world would have ever thought about the dear Lord throwing a wall of fire around about me?" And then I said in my heart, "There is not a devil in the pit or out of it that can hide in the brush and shoot a fellow in the back, for if the Lord is a wall of fire around about this man, the Devil could not make a bullet that could pierce that wall." Then I said, "There is not a devil in the universe that could get in a back alley on a dark night and stab a fellow in the back, for God is a wall of fire around about him." Then he also said that, He would be the glory in the midst thereof.

This glory in the midst is evidently the life that shines into the heart of man, it's an indwelling, internal, glowing, burning, sparkling, consuming fire that purges out dross, cleanses and purifies the nature, and keeps a man holy and clean. It is also the same light that is referred to by one of the other divine writers when he said, "Thy word is a lamp unto my feet, and a light unto my path." In a sense it is a miniature "pillar of fire by night and pillar of the cloud by day." When God led Israel out of bondage, He put a great pillar of fire and cloud both day and night, but He was then leading an army of probably two or three million people, and a pillar of cloud and fire to lead one man need not be nearly so large as one to lead millions.

But just as truly the light that lit up the path for the Israelites and blinded the eyes of the Egyptians is the very same thing to us today. Pharaoh and his host are a type of the Devil, and while God gave light to His people, the same light was so blinding and bewildering to the Egyptians that God hindered them in their progress. The same thing with us, the glory of God in the midst of us makes it dark and bewildering to the Devil.

That is one reason why the Devil does so many foolish things when he is trying to defeat one of God's children. It is often the case that the very thing that the devil does to defeat a saint proves to be the best thing for the saint and the worst thing for the Devil. Many of the schemes that the Devil gets up to defeat the saint of God prove to be a booster to the saint, and a great hindrance to the Devil himself. It is made plain in Ezekiel's vision, he saw a wheel within a wheel, and it seemed that the inner wheel was on fire, the sparks were flying in every direction, which means that out from the glory there is a power that will throw a circle of light and protection around a man for a hundred feet in every direction. Isaiah calls it a "way within a way," while Ezekiel calls it "a wheel within a wheel."

18

Guided by His Eye

JUST A WORD TO the sons and daughters of Adam, as I suppose just about everybody now believes that Adam and Eve were our grandfather and grandmother. Well, of course, the crowd that believes that we came from the tadpole probably would resent that statement, so as I am very broad and liberal I will allow the plug hat brigade to keep their own record. But here is what I want to talk to you about. I have just read in the 32d Psalm and 8th verse the wonderful words of the Lord. Notice them: "I will guide thee with mine eye." Well, thank the Lord! How beautiful it is in the Lord to be willing to guide us with His eye. In the days in which we live the very land is flooded with new "isms" and "schisms," new doctrines and heresies, and wildfire, fanaticism, religious crooks and bums, religious downs and outs, thousands of them morally too crooked to sleep in the roundhouse. They are too crooked to build a rail fence. They are not even straight enough to look at the rainbow. Many of them are as slick as eels, and as squirmy as water-moccasins. But they have just had a new revelation from the Lord, and they have just struck a new religious craze and now they are out in full blast to deliver the goods.

But we are not surprised at the new heresies when we see the dead formality in the church, for dead formalism breeds heresy. In these awful days to realize that God will guide us through this troublesome world with His eye is a consolation to us that ought to make us shout for the next thousand years. And with this wonderful text before us, it is too late now in the history of the world for a man to say he doesn't know where to go and what to believe, for we have it in the above declaration that God put Himself on record and has declared emphatically that He will guide us with His eye. I believe from the depth of my soul that I have been able to get to the right place at the right time and in the right way for the past forty years now, for just forty years ago I met Jesus on the frontiers of Texas, and He kicked the Devil out of my heart, and pitched him over the back yard fence, and set up His kingdom in my soul, and gave me such a chunk of sunshine and glory that I have been climbing over it and finding new things and beautiful things in my chunk of sunshine for the last forty years, and when I think of the fact that God is still guiding me with His eye, I have nothing to fear, nothing to lose, nothing to be uneasy about, just walk as Jesus walked and rest and abide in Him, and His will is my will, and the way that He has provided for me is so much better than I could have provided for myself, that it almost tickles me to death to think that I have so much in my favor.

The reader will remember that upon one occasion Jesus said to the broken-hearted disciples as He was leaving them, "When the Holy Ghost is come he will guide you into all truth." But away back before that the psalmist had said that, "I will guide you with mine eye." When a man is guided with the eye of the Lord, he will get to the place that God intended him to go to just exactly on time, and he will fit into the place when he gets there, just like the stripes fit in the rainbow. God looked in the direction that He wanted me to go, then He looked at me, and I hit the trail a-running, and thank the Lord, for these forty years, by being led by His Spirit, upheld by His hand, protected by a wall of fire, and guided by His eye, I have been able to keep off of the breakers. Many have been the plans that the Devil has laid to defeat and wreck me, but just as often as the Devil laid a plan to defeat me, God laid a plan to protect me, and when the Devil stepped up and laid down a temptation before me, Jesus walked up and laid down a way of escape by the side of it, and the Holy Spirit whispered in my soul, "This is the way, walk ye in it." And by listening to His voice and obeying His commands, thank God, I stand before Him today with His wings over my head, with His everlasting arms beneath me, and with His love in my soul. It is beautiful, it is glorious, it is beyond description. It looks like it is too good to be true, but thank God, it is so.

19

In the Hollow of His Hand

BELOVED SAINTS, IN STUDYING the 33rd chapter of the Book of Exodus, we find that Moses and the Lord carried on a very beautiful conversation, and finally it seemed that Moses was in such close relationship with God that he asked the Lord one day to show him His glory. At once the Lord notified Moses that no man could see His face and live, but Moses insisted on seeing the glory of God. Finally God told Moses that he could stand on a rock and His goodness would pass by, but that didn't seem to satisfy Moses. It seems from this wonderful chapter that he was urging his claim. At last the Lord told Moses that He would put him in a cleft in the rock and He would cover him there with His hand and that the trail of his garments would pass by and Moses might see His back, or His hinder parts. I suppose that this was one of the most beautiful sights that man has ever beheld on this earth. Nothing could be more beautiful. Just think of a man hid in the cleft of the rock with the hand of God himself over him, and the dazzling glory of God's presence passing by.

One day while talking to the Lord about being hid away in the hollow of His hand, I asked the Lord what it meant to be kept in the hollow of His hand, and this beautiful thought came into my mind. I feel that it was ordered of the Lord. He had me take a clean handkerchief out of my pocket and fold it up in my hands and cover it over until you couldn't see the handkerchief at all. And the Lord showed me as I would have a hard test and be peeled and scaled and blistered by the Devil, the Lord would have me to just raise up my hand and look in at the handkerchief. Of course it would be perfectly clean and white, and the Lord would say, "There is no mud on it yet." Then He would have me close it again, and then I would go through another hard test and the Lord would have me raise up my hand, and He would say, "There is no mud on it yet." But finally it seemed that the mud was getting mighty close, and it seemed that the mud was even thrown all over my hands but yet while the mud was flying thick and fast and it seemed that I was right on the very brink of darkness and many things were published in a certain journal, I was branded as a traitor and a liar and hypocrite and adulterer and scoundrel and so many things by one paper that was published in the United States.

But one day while the mud was flying the thickest the Lord seemed to just raise up His hand and look in at me and say, "My boy, there is no mud on you yet." "Lord, don't you see the mud flying?" and the Lord said, "Yes, but it hasn't touched you, and the mud was all thrown on My hand." And I said, "Glory be to God, if that is what it means to be kept in the hollow of Thy hand, I will never again fear the black hand of the Devil, and no abuse or misrepresentation will ever again cause me to even feel sad or feel that I have been injured in any way." And from that hour I have been perfectly willing to be kept in the hollow of God's hand. Bless His name!

20

Graven on the Palms of His Hands

To the saints and faithful in Christ Jesus: Greetings to you from Isaiah 49th chapter 16th verse. Well now, beloved, it might be profitable to you and me to just read Isaiah 49th chapter 16th verse and see what a wonderful statement that inspired man has left here on the pages of sacred history. Listen to His words: "Behold I have graven thee on the palms of my hands; thy walls are continually before me." Beloved, for a number of years I quoted that Scripture and I thought it said that our names were graven on the palms of His hands and I so quoted that for a number of years. But to my surprise, I read it one day as it really is, and it said, "Behold I have graven thee on the palms of my hands," and for a few minutes I was disappointed in the reading of this wonderful verse, but when I had time to think for a moment, I saw that there are hundreds and thousands of people by the same name, but there are no two that look alike. For instance, I know of two Henry Morrisons, and two Will Huffs, and two Jim Joneses, and at least a half dozen John Smiths but there are no two who look alike.

If it had said, "our names" we might have gotten into trouble at the judgment day, for every one of us would have thought, it was me. But when I saw the wonderful, wonderful thought, "Behold I have graven thee on the palms of my hands" it made my very heart leap for joy to think that God didn't have to look over at Texas or down in Mexico or over in England to find me. He just looks on the palms of His hands and sees me there, and when I thought of it in that light my heart was made to leap for joy. Of course there are people by my name, but no man can stand up at the judgment and say that he is me, and their names will cut no figure in the case. They might change my name after I got to heaven, but that doesn't matter after I am there myself. It matters not what they call me just so they call me in time to get in. There is so much difference between a man and his name. It makes but little difference as to what you call him, but what he is means everything.

And today I rejoice in the fact that God has graven us on the palms of His hands that I think when I see myself on God's hand at the judgment day that I will have enough to shout over for a million years. It will be something like a man beholding his own face in a looking glass, and thank the Lord there we can shine and shout forever. And then we remember the words of the Lord Jesus when He said upon one occasion, referring to His disciples, and the fact that the Devil was trying to destroy them. Christ said, "No man shall pluck them out of my hands." That gives us pretty much the same idea as the vision of Isaiah. He evidently saw us graven on the palms of the hands of God the Father. And now the blessed Christ comes along and tells us that no man or power, sinners or devils, can pluck a true disciple out of His hand. I have heard people refer to this and use it as a Scripture that taught the impossibility of falling away but there is no Scripture here that teaches that a man could not cast himself away if he desired, but it does teach that no man or Devil can take me out of God's hand and destroy me over my protest.

We know the Devil is a mighty Devil, but we know the Devil hasn't power enough to make any man in the world do wrong if the man has no desire to do wrong. The Devil may tempt a man and that is as far as he can go with it. The temptation may be a fierce one, but even that doesn't say I have to yield, for Jesus has said that "With every temptation I will make a way for your escape," and then He said emphatically that "I will not suffer you to be tempted above that ye are able to bear." Bless God, when the artilleries of hell are turned loose on me, all heaven is ready to stand by me and back me up.

No man has to do wrong if he doesn't want to, for which I say, Amen and glory to God in the highest. Beloved, just think of it; God has grace enough, power enough, love enough, and sympathy enough for us to so fill us and undergird us, and uphold us, that there is not a devil in the pit that can come over on God's territory and capture us and take us over on his side of the fence, unless we ourselves desire to go over, and bless God, the more I know about God, the less I care about the Devil, and the more I see in righteousness and holiness and perfect love, the less I see in this old world and the plans and schemes of the Devil. The best that the Devil has ever been able to get up is awfully poor dope. He can get up lying and stealing and cussing and drinking and fighting and adultery. That is one line of sin in a low, vile order. But he can get up other plans such as secret orders, fraternities, circuses, shows, theaters, ballrooms, card parties, big suppers, moving picture reels, big blow-outs in general and the best construction you can put on it, it produces fret and worry, sorrow, sadness, and disappointment, and none of it has ever satisfied a human soul, and it never can and never will, but bless God, you think of a man graven on the palms of God's hands and with the beautiful promise that no man or devil can pluck us out of the hands of Jesus. Brother, we have something that is worth paying the taxes on. This is worth holding on to with a death grip. Bless God, I have got my eye on the road, and I am scratching gravel toward heaven. Amen! Bless His name! We've got the goods.

21

The Ideal Church

No DOUBT THE READERS of this book have heard a thousand times, and people of about every faith and order, talk about the ideal church, and you have often wondered what kind of a church it was. Well, if you will listen to me a minute I believe I can tell you just exactly what kind of a church an ideal church is. God has given a whole Bible to a whole world, and in this Bible we find that God has provided a salvation from all sin for all men, provided through the atoning blood of a crucified Savior, and now an ideal church is a church where the pastor preaches a whole Bible, and where the preacher himself is red-hot, for God said His ministers were a flame of fire.

Again, God's ideal Sunday school superintendent in this ideal church is a man that is in perfect harmony with the Bible, and with his pastor, and he is in perfect harmony with the atoning blood of Jesus Christ, so that makes the Sunday school superintendent blood-red; and the Sunday school teachers in such a church would be a band of bloodwashed saints, and of course they would be snow-white and so filled with love and grace and glory that it would be perfectly easy for them to impart Bible truths to their classes. And in an ideal church the official board is so upright in their dealings with their fellow-man that their very lives might be said to be sky-blue, and the members of such a church as this would be as straight as a gun-stick. And there would be so much glory in their souls that it would be continually shining through their faces until you could take a rag and wipe enough heaven off of the faces of such a pastor, Sunday school superintendent, teachers, and official board and membership that it would put sinners under conviction throughout the length and breadth of their community.

Then of course there would be a revival of old-time, heart-felt, Holy Ghost religion in that church the year round. And such a company would give one-tenth of their income to the Lord, and there would always be money in the treasury to pay all the running expenses of the church. There would never be such a thing heard of as a church entertainment; there would be no broken china, and no lost spoons, and no ice cream freezers to carry back home, and of course there would never be such a thing as a church fuss, and from such an institution would go out pastors and evangelists, and missionaries to all quarters of the earth would be sent out by such a body of believers.

Such a church as this would be an ideal church. And while probably you never saw one just like that, you have seen some people in probably every church that you know anything about that were just such people as we have described, and you can see at a glance if every member in every church were like a few that you do know, we would have such a church as we have just described. And this brings up another thought. We know that it is God's plan to save the world through the church, and every honest, thinking, serious man will have to admit that God can not save the world through a worldly church. And that proves that it is God's plan to save the world through a holy church, and the hope of the world today is in the church.

The hope of the church is in the amount of holiness it has in it, and the danger of the church is in the amount of worldliness it has in it. And it is more than likely that every division that has ever been in the church was brought about because of a division in the church that was produced by worldliness in some and holiness in others. For holiness and worldliness have never gotten along and never will. Therefore they can never be brought in harmony with each other and can never work together, for the object of holiness is to leaven the whole lump and land them on the shores of eternal bliss, while the object of worldliness is to leaven the whole lump and sink the whole cargo into the pit of outer darkness. So, bless God, I am pulling for and hoping for an ideal church on earth. While I may never see one that everything in it is ideal, bless God, I have seen some that had some ideal members, and, bless God, that is encouraging.

22

The Two Greatest Powers

TO THE INTERESTED READER, and to the man or woman that desires to think a little for yourselves, and of course we all desire to do that:

No man wants to use the other man's head all the time, and almost everybody desires to use his own head part of the time. And in studying and reading my Book I found out these facts until it is perfectly clear to me that the two greatest powers that are known to God, men, or devils is just simply nothing more nor less than holiness and worldliness. While many things have been written on the subject yet we have by no means exhausted this subject.

The hope of the world as well as the hope of the church is in scriptural holiness, and the danger of the world as well as the danger of the church is in worldliness. It looks like we are hard pressed for words when we say it is dangerous for a worldly man or woman to be worldly, and yet that is the very thing we need. The Book said that "the sinner is in the world," and He said that the world will love its own. We see that is true. A gambler can go to town and find a gambling house before sundown. A drunkard can go to town and find a bootlegger before bedtime. A safecracker can go to town and locate a bank before he goes to supper, and an adulterer can go to town and locate a den of vice before the day is over. They seem to know each other, and work to each other's hand, and that within itself proves the awful danger is seen in the fact that the world in which they are is the very thing that will destroy them. And there is no power that can save a man from worldliness but the one thing that we call scriptural holiness.

Bishop Joyce said that holiness was God's proposition to get the Devil out of man. He never said a truer thing than that. We have seen men and women who have gone to the bottom in downright worldliness but they would weep their way to the altar, unload the affairs of this life and the old world, in such a way that they were born again and taken out of the world, and . maybe a few weeks later the same person would be cleansed and purified and made holy. And then they had been taken out of the world, and the world had been taken out of them, and while they were in a sense in the world, yet they were not of the world, and they were as free from worldliness as if they had never been mixed up with it. So worldliness has power enough in it to wreck, ruin, blight, blast, mildew, and damn the soul. While holiness has power enough to undo everything in the human heart that sin and the Devil and the world has done for him and lift him above the whole thing and make him a fit subject to keep company with the angels and walk and talk with God.

23

The Whole Lamb

IN THE 12TH CHAPTER of Exodus we find that when Moses was preparing to take the Israelites out of the land of bondage that he outlined a number of things they must do, in order to leave bondage. Among the things he said to do, one thing was he said they were to take a whole lamb. As the reader will notice, this lamb was to be a type of Christ, for it was used in the Passover. And the Passover, of course, refers to the coming of the blessed Son of God. You will see at a glance that they had to take a whole lamb, and not a part of one.

Sad to say, the American church has reached the place where the lamb has been much divided. Some denominations can take His death while others take His life, some take His beautiful example, others His beautiful personality, but just as stubbornly reject His blood, and His dying groans and sweat and agony on Golgotha's brow. Many seem to admire His beautiful life, but are ashamed of His death on the cross. Some stubbornly reject His divinity, some deny His eternal Sonship, some do not desire to look back so far as His eternal deity, they want something more modern and up-to-date. They reject almost everything that is written in the Book concerning the Christ. Here is one point that will illustrate what I mean: Not long ago in one of my campmeetings a great preacher stood on the platform and made this fearful statement. Here are his exact words: "The church of which I am a member has taken the fire out of hell, and the gold out of heaven, and the blood out of the atonement, and the inspiration out of the Scriptures, and God out of Christ." If he was correct in his statement concerning the teachings of his church, nothing could be sadder than what he told that great multitude of people.

And now for a few minutes I want to show you that when a man rejects the deity of Jesus Christ and only accepts His personality, he has cut himself off from the kingdom of Jesus Christ and he is adrift on the sea of time like a lost vessel without a chart or compass. For every Scripture that the man uses to prove the personality of Jesus Christ, we heartily accept, and take the same Scriptures also and prove that Jesus Christ was not only a man but that He was God. First, they tell us that Jesus Christ stood at the grave of Lazarus and wept, and that that proves Him to be just a man. But they seem to forget that the blessed Christ not only wiped the tears of His beautiful eyes as a man, but He spoke the life-giving word and said, "Lazarus, come forth," and immediately the man that was dead and bound in the tomb now stands in the presence of that multitude wonderfully alive. So if Jesus was a man when He wept, He was a God when He called the dead man out of the grave.

Again, they tell us that Jesus was a man because He stood on the mountain-side and preached the gospel, and that proves Him, they say, to be a man. We gladly accept that statement, but in the same hour He looked up to heaven and gave thanks and took five barley loaves and two little fish and brake them and handed them to the great multitude and with this prayer and thanksgiving at what we would call the dinner table, Jesus Christ proves Himself to be God, for with the small quantity of food He fed five thousand men beside the women and children. If His preaching on the mountain-side proves Him to be a man, His feeding the multitude proves Him to be a God. Now don't forget these two wonderful facts that we find in this lesson, and they both took place within one day and probably within one hour of each other.

The first thing I want you to remember is that Jesus Christ preached like a man; the second thing is that He multiplied bread and fish like a God. Again the people tell us that they know Jesus was a man because He went out on the mountain-side on another occasion and spent many of the dark hours of the night in prayer. They tell us that that proves Him to be a man, for God never goes to the hills and holds prayermeetings. But they seem to have overlooked the fact that while Jesus was on the mountain-side in prayer that His disciples were in the middle of the Sea of Galilee in a little boat and a fearful storm was raging, and at a late hour of the night the blessed Son of

God rose from His knees and walked down that beautiful mountain slope until He came to the raging sea, and now behold Him as He walked over those raging waves as though He was stepping on cement blocks. The reader will have to admit that if the Son of God prayed like a man on the mountain-side He walked the raging waves of the sea like a God. So we accept these two facts and rejoice in them both, that He prayed like a man on the mountain-side but walked the waves of Galilee like a God. If one proves His personality the other proves His divinity.

Again they tell us that they know He was a man because on another occasion they were crossing the Sea of Galilee, and it seemed that the Son of God was tired, and manlike He laid down on a pillow in the back part of the little ship and went to sleep. We are told that He was a man because they say God never takes a nap, therefore Jesus was only a man. But we would have the critic to know He was more than a man even upon this occasion, for while the little boat rocked and the Son of God slept, a dark cloud swept down over the Judean hills, and it seemed the storm hung heavy over that little sea, but evidently the Devil was too well posted to believe he could destroy a boat with the Son of God in it. Nevertheless the storm swept down over Galilee and while the waves were raging the disciples became excited; they hurried to their sleeping Master and shook Him and said, "Master, carest thou not that we perish?" And He arose and rebuked the winds and immediately every blue breaker went back into his hole and put away their white caps and they behaved themselves as though they knew that their Creator had arrived on the scene. To any thinking mind these two facts prove not only the personality of the Son of God, but His divinity. If He slept like a man which He did, and we believe and rejoice in it, and we might say, if that was a man that was taking a nap, who was that that commanded the storm and the sea? It will be plain to the reader that nobody but God can command a storm and a raging sea, and immediately receive from them strict obedience. Beloved, if that doesn't prove that Jesus Christ was the divine Son of God, and He has all power in heaven and in earth there is no use to look for facts either in the Bible or out of it.

Again, they tell us that they know that Jesus Christ was just a man because that after His boat had landed on the coast of the Gadarenes Jesus came out of the boat and sat down on the bank and had a little conversation with a gentleman that had a legion of devils in him, but the reader must remember that there is nothing there to prove He wasn't a God, for even the devils in the demoniac cried out and said, "Art thou come hither to torment us before the time?" They seemed to know Jesus Christ, and they asked of Him to grant them a request. You say, "What was their request?" Well, it is there in the Book to be found by any man who wants to read it. They asked Him if He cast them out of the man if He would permit them to go into a herd of swine that were feeding on the mountain-side, and Jesus granted them their request. And then they seem to forget that this demoniac had been a terror to that country. He had been bound with all kinds of fetters. He had snapped them off like twine strings. He was a raving madman, a terror to a country, but thank the Lord, after one meeting with the Son of God we see him next clothed and in his right mind and sitting at the feet of Jesus. A few minutes ago he was a demonized, raving maniac, but thank God a few minutes later he was clothed, and in his right mind, and a perfect Christian gentleman. We will thank God till our dying day that Jesus went to that village and cast the legion of devils out of that poor soul.

But we see another picture here that to us is very sad. No sooner had the devils been cast out of the man and they enter the hogs and they run down the hill and perished in the sea, the reader will notice that the owners of the hogs came out and they besought Jesus to leave their coasts, and Jesus left and as far as we have been able to find, He never returned to that community. But thank God, He went and gave them one exhibition of His power and glory. It would seem that the sinners and the devils believe that Jesus Christ was God. The devils believed him to be, and we are persuaded that the sinners did also, because they wanted Him to depart. And we know that they believed He was more than man, for in His first visit to their town He handled a man that they had never been able to handle. Thank God, it is just so today. All the cases that are unmanageable by man are manageable by the Son of God. He has met lots of men that in the eyes of their neighbors are hard customers, but Jesus broke their fetters, pardoned their guilt, cleansed their hearts, filled them with the Holy Ghost, made them clean and pure and Christed men, when everybody else had given them up.

The reader will remember here that we started out with the fact that we must take a whole lamb; don't let any of us forget that while it may be possible that some of the great preachers all around you are trying to convince their congregations that Jesus was a good man but no more divine than they themselves, that they are evidently the crowd Jesus referred to when He described some one as a wolf with a sheepskin on him. We are afraid that crowd is increasing, at least it would seem so to a man who travels and looks and listens.

The Lamb without Blemish

We want to talk to you a few minutes about this wonderful lamb that was used in the Passover the night that the Israelites left Egyptian bondage. God said of the lamb that it was to be without blemish. The word blemish here refers to the physical structure of the lamb. You will notice the lamb could not have been blind or crippled or one-eyed or even bob-tailed, or a nick out of his ear. The reason for that is the lamb was a type of Christ. At a glance the reader will see why God required a lamb with a perfect body, for a deformed lamb could not properly represent Christ. In proof of that, if the reader will turn to 1st Peter, 1st chapter and 18th, 19th, and 20th verses, we have this remarkable statement: Peter said, "Forasmuch as ye know that ye were not redeemed with corruptible things as silver and gold from your vain conversation, received by the tradition from your fathers, but with the precious blood of Christ as of a lamb without blemish and without spot, who verily was foreordained before the foundation of the world but was manifest in these last times for you." The reader will see the marks of similarity between the lamb of the Passover and Christ. They were both without blemish, they are both called "The Lamb," they both were to lay down their lives by the shedding of their blood. And the lamb in the Passover being without blemish is one of the most beautiful types of Christ given in the Old Testament history.

Here we might help the reader some by adding two quotations, one from the Old Testament, and one from the new. When Abraham was going to the mountain with his boy Isaac to offer him as a sacrifice to God we read in the 22d chapter of Genesis, that Isaac said to his father, "Where is the lamb?" The reader will remember that Abraham said to Isaac, "My son, God will provide himself a lamb." Then we notice again in the 1st chapter of John that when John the Baptist saw Jesus Christ coming to Jordan to receive baptism at his hands, John the Baptist pointed to Christ and said, "Behold the Lamb of God that taketh away the sin of the world." How strange it would seem that a question of such importance as was asked by Isaac was unanswered for nineteen hundred years. For the reader will remember that Isaac said, "Where is the lamb?" and John said, "Behold the Lamb!" But between the question and the answer nearly two thousand years rolled by, and Isaac's question could not be answered until Jesus came, for Jesus was the fulfilling of the question that was asked by Isaac.

A Church without Blemish

Now, beloved, as we have been talking about a lamb without blemish and a Christ without blemish, we next notice that we are to have a church without blemish, for the reader is perfectly familiar with the fact that the Church is the Bride, the Lamb's wife, and as truly as the Bridegroom is to be without blemish at once we will notice that He would expect His Bride to be like Himself. Therefore we have the wonderful statement in the 5th chapter of Ephesians in the 25th, 26th, and 27th verses. One of the most remarkable statements in some respects that are found in the writings of the great apostle. Here it is: "Husbands love your wives even as Christ also loved the church and gave himself for it that he might sanctify and cleanse it with the washing of water by the word that he might present it to himself a glorious church not having spot or wrinkle or any such thing but that it should be holy and without blemish." Here the reader will see that not only the lamb was without blemish and Christ was without blemish, but in this last quotation we see that the Church, the Lamb's wife, is to be without blemish. It is perfectly natural for the bridegroom to desire a bride that is as pure and holy as himself, and who could blame him? For any man that is worthy to be called a man wants a wife that is pure and holy and clean and spotless. He also wants a wife that will love him perfectly. This he has a right to demand. And while that is true of the husband it is also true of the bride; she also desires a husband that is as pure and as holy and clean and spotless as she herself. And this she has a perfect right to demand.

Now we know that the Church has such a Bridegroom in the person of Jesus Christ, but if we are to take the American church as the Bride of Christ, we see a great difference between the Bride and the Bridegroom. For the great bulk of the members of the American church are holiness rejecters, and sad to say, many of them are sin accepters. They are ashamed to dance before the Lord, but are not ashamed to dance before the Devil. They would be ashamed to shout in the church, but are not ashamed to shout for baseball. Often they are so busy with the ballroom and euchre parties that they have neglected the night of prayers, and so you can get ten out on a Wednesday night to pray and five hundred out on Thursday night to eat doughnuts. So we see that while the Bridegroom is away preparing a mansion for His Bride, that the Bride has gone to flirting with another man, which to be real plain, the Church of Jesus Christ has yoked up with the world, but we remember the text says that the Bride was to be a glorious Bride. She is to be without spot, that means that she has no defect or blemish in her moral character. When He said, "She is to be holy," that means she is to be delivered from all sin both actual and inbred, and then He said she is to be without wrinkle. Wrinkle refers to age, and the Bride of Christ will never grow old, for there are no old people in heaven. Our souls will always be young, and one of the divine writers said that we are to be as fair as the sun and as clear as the moon and as terrible as an army with banners, and he said of this beautiful Bride that she looketh forth as the morning. If she is as clear as the sun, there will be nothing below the board, but the life of His Bride will be open and above board, she is not only to be as clear as the sun but as fair as the moon. The moon borrows her light and glory from the sun of the solar system, and the Bride of Christ receives her light and glory from the Sun of righteousness. We used to sing, "The moon shines bright, and the stars give good light," and always denotes a courtship, and we used to say that a boy that can take a young lady to church on Sunday night down a beautiful sandy road on a moonlight night and not make love to her is an awfully poor excuse for a man. And we find Christ wonderfully in love with His Bride, so much so that we read He suffered without the gate that He might sanctify and make the Church holy in order that He might present her to Himself, a glorious Bride.

The Lamb Roast with Fire

Beloved saints, the Lord bless every one of you nearly to death and set the sideboards of your soul out and make you a bread wagon, and load you up with bread from the King's table, and as you run over the roots and rocks of life may a few loaves fall off for the hungry multitudes. If that will take place, which it ought to, you will be able to toll a great multitude right into the kingdom of our Lord Jesus Christ, for it is a fact that pigs will follow a loaded wagon when the corn is tumbling off, and we ought to be able to do as well by the people as we have done by the pigs, and thank the Lord we will do it. Now for a little while let's you and I study a beautiful thought which is brought out in this wonderful 12th chapter of Exodus, for Moses said, "Your lamb shall be roast with fire." The lamb had to be roasted with fire before it was ready to serve, and just so with us; we must have the fire from heaven on us before we are prepared to serve. The man that hasn't been burned out is still woefully in need of something from the Lord. But thank the Lord, John the Baptist said in the 3d chapter of Matthew, that "He shall baptize you with the Holy Ghost and with fire," and when the refining fire goes through our hearts and inbred sin is burned out, and the old man is crucified, and the "body of sin" is destroyed, and the fire begins to burn on the altar of our soul, it won't be long until there will be somebody sticking out both hands and all their toes as they warm by your fire. If we have fire enough to warm the people, we will be able to burn our way through the difficulties, and surrounding circumstances, and the imaginary impossibilities that the Devil will throw across our pathway. For the Devil is a world-beater on showing weak saints dangerous things that are really not in existence. The most of our troubles have been brought about by troubles that never existed. The average man sees the bridge break down before he is within two miles of the creek, and he just knows that he will never be able to cross the bridge and behold, when he gets to the place where the bridge looked so dangerous, there is nothing in existence there. But thank the Lord, if we get the fire to burning right good, we will he able to burn our way through anything that the Devil can scare up. But don't forget we are no good until we get the fire from heaven. I want to praise the Lord that the fire still burns and the wheel still turns, and God is still dropping me off at the right place. Bless His name!

Put Away all Leaven from Among You

We are told again in this wonderful 12th chapter of Exodus that the Israelites were to put away all leaven from among them, and they were to receive the lamb with unleavened bread, and the Lord told them emphatically they could not keep any leaven in the house and receive the lamb. The reason for that was, that leaven is a type of sin, and no man can receive Christ, and keep any sin in his house, or rather in his heart. All leaven had to be put away. Leaven is that peculiar thing that we put in the biscuit dough. It is commonly called yeast nowadays, but it is the same thing that was called leaven in those early days. And you can put a small amount of yeast in a piece of biscuit dough and heat the dough to a certain degree of heat and the yeast will cause it to swell to several times the size that it was before the yeast went to work. We have often had people tell us after they had had a spell of anger and the "Old Man" had gotten up in them and turned over, that they had had an uprising, and how true to life it was. The reader can see at a glance that the yeast was at work, and when you see a man sweating and puffing and swaggering, with his face red and his nose white, with his teeth clenched, you may know at once that the yeast is now doing its work, for you can see now that the dough is several times larger than it was. How true to the spiritual condition are these facts. For they say themselves when they are cooling off that they sure did get hot. Well, don't forget that the biscuit dough has to get hot before the yeast can or will do its work. And when the dough gets as hot as it has to be to start the yeast there is always a mighty upheaval, and we are not surprised that they call it an uprising.

Occasionally we hear a preacher tell us from the pulpit that leaven stands for grace, and that the little grace we get in conversion will work up and work out and work through until the whole is leavened, and try to make it appear that the yeast stands for grace. But, beloved, that couldn't be, for the reader will remember that at the opening of this chapter the Lord told Israelites to put away all leaven from among them before they could receive the lamb, and it would seem strange that leaven would stand for grace, and a man would have to put it all away from him in order to receive Christ. Again, when we come to think it over, leaven could not stand for grace because a sinner has no grace in him, and the reader will remember that in the 5th chapter of 1st Corinthians and the 6th and 7th verses St. Paul said to the church at Corinth, "Your glorying is not good, know ye not that a little leaven leaveneth the whole lump?" then notice in the very next clause he says, "Purge out therefore the old leaven that ye may be a new lump, as ye are unleavened, for even Christ our passover is sacrificed for us." Here the reader will see that if the leaven in the 6th verse is grace, Paul himself tells them in the 7th verse to get rid of it, using almost the same language that Moses had used in talking to the Israelites in the 12th chapter of Exodus, proving to the mind of any reader that leaven could not stand for grace.

But it is amazing nowadays how some men have tried to twist the Book in order to dodge facts, and to cover up truth. Here is one point: a big preacher in one of the western cities preached on the "more excellent way," using the 31st verse of the 12th chapter of 1st Corinthians as his text in which he showed the people that the more excellent way that the apostle was going to show these Corinthian Christians, meant our beautiful boulevards and fine road systems of America, and the riding in automobiles, and showed that the difference between the rough roads in early days where our forefathers traveled in ox wagons, while any thinking man or woman in any church or faith knows perfectly well that the more excellent way there that the apostle describes was nothing short of the beautiful experience of perfect love as described in the 13th chapter of 1st Corinthians, and yet this gentleman was honored with that wonderful title of D.D. In his case evidently D.D. meant Dead to truth and Delivered to the Devil. All Christians enjoy good roads and a ride in an automobile. These are great blessings but have nothing to do with the above Scripture in this world, and couldn't have. The Apostle Paul had no reference to macadamized roads or automobiles when he wrote this wonderful text to the church at Corinth.

Thank the Lord we little folks have found out what the old apostle meant. He wanted these people who were so dear to his old heart to be sanctified wholly, and filled with the blessed Holy Ghost, and made perfect in love. Nothing short of that would satisfy the Apostle Paul, or the man that is writing this book. And I want to say right here, bless God, I have got it, and the fire is burning in my soul, and the old leaven is purged out and there is no uprising there today. Glory be to God the Father, Son, and Holy Ghost! Amen, and amen! If the Devil was to just stick his nose through the crack of my theological fence, bless God, I would have another shouting spell. Hallelujah to the name of Jesus! How wonderful it is to know Jesus in His blessed fullness and His beautiful companionship, and His great loving face out before us with His everlasting arms beneath us, and our souls on the stretch for the home in the glory land. I can say with the old saints, "It is better felt than told." No man can describe it, but all can enjoy it.

Receiving the Lamb with Bitter Herbs

We find again in this remarkable chapter that the Israelites were to receive the lamb with bitter herbs. Now in the preceding chapter we showed you that they had to put away all leaven in order to receive the lamb, and we notice in this chapter that they had to receive the lamb with bitter herbs. It is very clear to the mind of the reader that bitter herbs in this connection stands for the doctrine of repentance. For no cup has ever been drunk by the heart of a penitent sinner that is as bitter as the cup of repentance, and this is one of the hard things in connection with getting rid of sin. No man loves to drink the bitter cup, but all will have it to do in order to find the Lamb. But it must be drunk to the bottom before Christ can he received. For the doctrine of repentance covers all the ground of straightening up the back track. It is a bitter cup to have to publicly confess our sins and forsake our sins and then take our back track and make restitution, and take back that which does not belong to us and beg pardon from both God and man, and that makes the cup a very bitter one.

There are plenty of people in the country who would get religion and go to heaven if they did not have to drink the cup of repentance, and as far as possible straighten up their past records, but it will have to be done. For God did not have Moses to preach one kind of doctrine to the Israelites and then preach a different doctrine to us, and the facts are that the Israelites could not receive the lamb without the bitter herbs, and neither can you and I. I used to hear the old Methodist preachers say in their prayers, "O Lord, I thank thee that we are on praying grounds and pleading terms with Thee." I thought in those days that that was a very common expression, but, beloved, that was my mistake, for that was a very uncommon expression, for no man ever uttered a greater statement than those old heroes uttered in that prayer. For no man is on praying grounds and pleading terms, as they called it, as long as he carries one unconfessed sin in his bosom or as long as he has one nickel in his possession that belongs to another; therefore, the old preacher meant more than we thought for when he thanked God he was on praying grounds. But any man that will drink the cup of repentance to the bitter dregs and swallow the bitter herbs can pray a hole through the skies, so big that the light of God's face will shine down through that hole and all over his soul until he will look like he is about half glorified, when the facts of it is he has just drunk the cup of repentance and prayed a hole through the skies and the light of God's countenance has lightened up his pathway from earth to glory. Beloved, that man is liable to have any kind of a religious spell at almost any time of the day, in almost any part of the world that he may be.

Receive the Lamb with Your Loins Girded

To the sons and daughters of the Almighty scattered abroad: We want to notice again some beautiful things from the 12th chapter of Exodus. Now Moses told the Israelites that they were to receive the lamb with their loins girded. At first this would seem to be a strange statement, but after looking at it more closely it will reveal its own self to you. This refers to the clothing that they were to wear. The oriental garment was a loose robe over their shoulders coming down to their ankles and when they were to make a journey they were to put a big leather girdle around their loins and gird themselves up, in order that it would pull the loose robe up about halfway between their ankle and knees. This was done in order that they might walk well. The girdle also would brace their back and loins and give them strength for their heavy march. The reader will remember that in the picture of the old family Bible of the pilgrims, they all had on this loose garment and the girdle around their loins, so you see the Israelites had to assume the role of a pilgrim before they could receive the lamb, and how true is that with us today. No man can receive Christ without becoming a pilgrim, and the old Book says that we are strangers and pilgrims here below, and that we are seeking a city which hath foundations whose builder and maker is God. We understand from the teaching of the Book that all truly regenerated people are pilgrims. But the Apostle Paul gave us some wonderful insights into the life of a pilgrim in that wonderful 11th chapter of Hebrews. He said of them that they wandered about in sheepskins and goatskins, were destitute, and afflicted, of whom he said, this world was not worthy. He said they wandered about in deserts and mountains and dens and caves of the earth and that they all died in the faith. Another remarkable fact in connection with their receiving the lamb with the loins girded was that they could not leave Egyptian bondage until they assumed the role of a pilgrim and received the lamb with their loins girded.

And what was true of the Israelites is just as true of us. For the child of God today is just as truly robed and girded and is running this remarkable race with his face set toward the celestial city as was the face of the Israelites set toward the land of Canaan. And a Christian is a very busy man. He is making tracks with the toes pointed toward the New Jerusalem; in fact, he has said good-by to this old world, and is so busy following the Lamb, that he has no time to ride the goat. He has his eye on the cross and is running for his life. It was hard on him to say good-by to all the goat-riders and these splendid gentleman of the cloth and take the lonely way with Jesus. He has no time for the entertainments and the great blow-outs of the world. His business is to scratch gravel. He has no time to look back, nor to stay on the plains. He is bound for the mountain-top of holiness and righteousness. Every move he makes is heavenward. He now has on his robe, his eye on the cross with a spring in his heel and a well in his soul, and his face is set like a flint. He is one of the most peculiar men on earth; not exactly in the way he is dressed but in the way he lives. For he lives different from the other man, for he is a citizen of another country. Amen!

Receiving the Lamb with Your Shoes on Your Feet

Beloved, we are now getting ready to put on our gospel shoes. For again we notice that Moses said to the Israelites that they were to receive the lamb with their shoes on their feet. We read in another place that Moses said that their shoes were to be iron and brass, so I am not surprised now when I think of it that the Israelites wore their shoes for forty years, and we nowhere read that they had to have them half-soled or new heels put on them. Well, beloved, think of a man with iron shoes on, how well protected he is. At a glance you can see that this man can wade through thorns and thistles and briars. He can climb over rocks and hills and mountains for years and never get a thorn in his toe nor a briar in his heel. And of course there is no danger of a man stumping off a toenail. If a great rattlesnake or a copperhead or a boa-constrictor or any of these dangerous reptiles that man has to fight along the path of life undertakes to bother a man with a pair of iron shoes on, he can stamp his head into the ground and mash it as flat as a pancake. There is no danger of a fellow getting snakebitten.

I thank the Lord that a man can have a pair of gospel shoes made out of iron, glory to God for such protection! Thank the Lord for the good things that are coming our way at last. Beloved, iron shoes are quite a fortune. In the next place, if a bulldog would come out of a fence corner and growl at a fellow with iron shoes on, he could simply kick that dog in the under jaw and turn him two double somersaults, and hand him a few good kicks in the short ribs that would open the eyes of that pup and let him realize at once that he had made the wrong choice, and that old warrior wouldn't be bothered any more with a bulldog soon.

Beloved, just think of what a dangerous weapon an iron shoe is to rattlesnakes and bulldogs, and what a wonderful protection they are to a pilgrim as he travels through this world. I wouldn't take anything in the world for mine. St. Paul one day looked down at his iron shoes and a big smile played up and down his face and he said, "Gentlemen, I am shod with the preparation of the gospel of peace," and he turned and said to me, "So run that ye may obtain," and I said, "Bless God, I am everlastingly at it."

Beloved, if a man can have such preparation as we find here offered to the saints, there is no reason in the world why we should hobble around and complain of the little difficulties of life, for a man that is so well shod as the pilgrims were need not fear the rough places of life. We have noticed that he was well clothed with his oriental garment on, and now with his gospel shoes, with his soul on a stretch for the glory land. There is no power on earth or in the pit of darkness that can keep the man from going through. There is no way to keep the Devil from tempting him, but there is no power that the Devil has that can make us yield. No man has to yield to the temptation of the Devil unless he wants to, for our heavenly Father has said, "I will not suffer you to be tempted above that ye are able to bear, but will with the temptation make a way of escape." We see from the above quotation that when the Devil comes up and throws down a temptation before you, that Jesus walks up and lays down the way of escape by the side of it, and so we will say praise God from whom all blessings flow, and buckle up our belt and put on our shoes and start for the race.

There is another interesting fact about this case and it is this, that no man will ever start anywhere until he puts on his shoes. As long as a man lays around in the morning barefooted until his wife gets breakfast, too lazy to knock the flies off his nose, and with barely enough life to knock the bumblebees off his toes, let it be remembered that that man will never get anything done, but you take the old boy that rolls out of bed at break of day and while he is shaking the sand out of his socks with one hand, he is knocking the mud off his heels with the other, that man is going to make a corn crop, and no make-believe about it, and what is true in the literal world is also true in the spiritual world. Amen! So get a move on you and let's meet at the marriage supper of the Lamb. But don't undertake to come without your shoes on, for if you do they won't let you in.

Receive the Lamb with the Staff in Your Hand

Now, beloved, church members and lovers of the gospel truth, we take fresh courage and take our staff in our hand and march to the battle's front, for we notice again in this wonderful 12th chapter of Exodus that Moses told the Israelites to receive the lamb with their staff in their hand. Now this staff was a big walking stick, we would judge about as big round as a man's wrist, and probably about five feet long. It was their protection. They didn't use firearms in those days as we do at present, but if a mountain lion came out of the woods and growled at one of those old Israelites when he had his staff in his hand, he could knock every tooth in his mouth right down his neck at one lick, and then beat him into a frazzle, and put his stick on his shoulder, and march on down the highway of holiness. This stick was a great source of joy and comfort to the man who carried it. When he was tired he could lean on his staff and rest, when he went up a mountain, he found it very useful, he could push himself up the hill and help himself over the slick places and rough cliffs. It was also just as useful when the fellow started down the mountain, he could often lean on his staff and hold himself back. He had two legs of his own, and his staff which was a kind of a third leg and meant so much to the travelers in those early days.

But in our day we now use for our staff God the Father, God the Son, and God the Holy Ghost. We lean on the triune Godhead. They protect us from the wild beasts along the highway. They help us to climb the mountains, they help us down the steep hills and when we are tired we lean on them. What would we do without this wonderful staff? It is a comfort to us by day and our protection by night. The old Book is often our walking stick, for as we read the Book, we walk and talk by the way. We draw our very spiritual life and existence from the Word of God through the power of the blessed Holy Ghost, which is sent to us by the Father and the Son. Thank God, we receive the Lamb with our staff in our hands.

Receive the Lamb in Haste

We notice again in this remarkable chapter that Moses told the Israelites to receive the lamb in haste. We understand by this that the time had come when they were to receive the lamb and leave bondage or reject the lamb and stay in Egypt. Egyptian bondage is a type of sin, so understood by the majority at least, of the Bible readers. Pharaoh is a type of the Devil, and Egyptian bondage a type of the work the Devil puts poor sinners to doing, for while the Israelites gathered straw and made brick and worked in the slime-pits under the lash of the taskmaster, they were then away from God's country and on the Devil's territory, and they were servants and serving their enemy, which is the most remarkable picture of the life of sin that is given in the Old Testament. Every man knows, that will think for a moment, that every sinner is serving his enemy, for the greatest enemy any sinner has ever had has been the Devil, and the only friend he ever had was Jesus, and yet, strange as it seems, sinners will serve the Devil and reject Jesus Christ. Now Moses had been planning for some time to leave Egyptian bondage with the Israelites, and the plan was to go into the land of Canaan which represents God's country, and the lamb had been killed, and the Passover was made ready, and finally the time came when they had stayed in Egypt their last day and up till the last night, and now they were to arise at once and go with Moses out of Egypt, or stay there and perish. His command was, "Receive the lamb in haste." This means to get up and get out of there. It meant, "Don't delay in your going, for every one that delayeth will perish."

It is just so with us today. The time comes when every man must give up sin and go with Jesus Christ or stay in sin and perish eternally. After reading and traveling and talking with people for years I am convinced that multiplied thousands of saints today received Christ on their very last call of mercy. The time came when they had their last call. They realized that God was giving them their last and final call to mercy; hence, we have heard them say by the thousands, "I just barely got in on my last chance." I am sure that they felt that way about it, and they felt truly that if they rejected Jesus Christ one more time He would never pay any more attention to them. In their testimony they have said publicly, "If I had rejected Jesus Christ one more time, it was so plain to me that I would never have another call to mercy that I fairly ran to the altar of prayer and begged God for the sake of my lost soul to have mercy."

Oh, beloved, multiplied thousands have gotten in on their last call. But think of the sad millions that have heard the call so often, and have turned a deaf ear so many times and said no to God and hardened their own hearts, stiffened their own necks, choked and stifled their own convictions that the blessed Holy Ghost had brought to their hearts until God left them, until today we have a nation of God-forgetters and Christ-despisers, and Holy Ghost rejecters, and sad as this statement may seem, God pays no more attention to them than if they had no soul. The buggy horse they drive has just as much conviction now as they have. You might say, "Why is this?" We answer the time came when they were to receive Christ in haste or reject Him and perish, and they shook their head for the last time at God, and God's dealings with them closed. In a few years or maybe a few weeks on their dying bed darkness will settle down over them, they will have no feelings, their friends may pray, they will show but little or no concern, their testimony will be, "I am lost," and the next dealing they will have with God will be at the judgment bar, for we remember the words of Jesus when He said to the Jews, "How often would I have gathered you together as a hen gathers her chickens under her wing, but ye would not, therefore your house is left unto you desolate, for I would and ye would not." So Jesus walked out of their temple and shook the dust from His feet as a testimony against them, and said, "Your house is left desolate." He never went back to it.

When I See the Blood I Will Pass Over You

Beloved, the last lesson we will give you from the 12th chapter of Exodus is on the blood. We read in this chapter that Moses said, "Ye shall strike the blood on the two side posts, and on the upper door posts," then he adds, "And when I see the blood I will pass over you." The blood of the lamb that was used in the Passover is a beautiful type of the blood of Christ. The lamb himself was a type of Christ and the lamb had to shed its blood before it could be used by the Israelites, and Christ had, to shed His blood before He could redeem a lost world. The blood of the lamb was to be the protection that was thrown around the Israelites, and this blood was to keep back the death angel from entering their home, for every person that did not have the blood on his front door posts, and upper posts, there was a corpse found in that home, and just as truly as the blood protected the Israelites, the blood of Jesus is to be the protection of His people in a world of sin, for it is through the blood of Jesus Christ that we are delivered from sin and the power of the Devil and delivered from eternal death. We even read in the Bible that the angels desire to look into this great salvation and that the songs of the redeemed in the holy city will be concerning the blood of the Son of God. The blood had to be put on the two side posts and the upper door posts as a public sign or example. The command was not to put it on the back posts of the door, on the door steps even, but it was to be put on the front door, and beloved, you can't imagine any old Israelite that night when the death angel was going through the land with a drawn sword leaving a corpse in every home, that any of those people that night would have been ashamed of the blood, and the greatest protection that ever came to a band of slaves was the blood of the lamb, and the little family was safe in his mud hut in the land of Goshen. Therefore that wonderful transaction that took place that night in the land of Egypt is called the Passover.

It was so named or called the Passover simply from the fact that the destroying angel passed over every house that had blood on the door. Again it pointed to the death and sufferings of Christ, when He too, should give up His life and shed His blood to redeem not only Israel but the whole world. And from the day of the shedding of the blood of Christ until this present hour all mankind can look back to the hill of Calvary and see a bleeding victim on the cross which means that there is a deliverance for me from my sin and bondage to the Devil. Thank the Lord, the blood will not only pardon the guilt that is found in the heart of a lost sinner, but will also cleanse and purify the heart of a justified believer. In trying to describe this great salvation we have often said that it was blood-red and snow-white and red-hot and sky-blue, and as straight as a gun-stick. We have used this language because we probably had no better language to use.

24

Riches

As everybody wants to make a fortune, and riches is the common talk of the day, we might put in a little time very profitably studying the beautiful things that our heavenly Father tells us in His Word about riches. People refer to this country and speak of it as their estate. We hear much about the great estate of some people, and while others are talking about their estate, we also are classed among those who are extremely rich. We range among the "upper tens," for you will understand we are going up later on. We even outrank what is supposed to be the "400." Thank God, there are millions of us! Now we just want to notice that the Bible speaks of "riches," and again we are told that we are to have "exceeding riches." In the third place He tells us that we are to have "great riches" and in the fourth place He reaches the climax by speaking of "unsearchable riches." No doubt in my mind but what the expression of "unsearchable riches" is the "fullness of the blessing" to such a degree that it could scarcely be improved upon in this world.

While it would be a difficult matter to explain unsearchable riches, thank God, it is wonderful to enjoy. Evidently the man with unsearchable riches is the man that has been cleaned up and then cleaned out and then filled up and sent out and charged and surcharged and wound up and then this fellow will have God for his Father and Jesus Christ for his Savior and the Holy Ghost for his abiding Comforter, and the redeemed saints of all the ages for his brothers and sisters. He will have the angels for his companions. The Bible will be his way-bill from earth to glory, and heaven will be his eternal home. This fellow you see is evidently well off. We think that these four expressions of riches are all to be found in this bill of fare, and we believe that riches, exceeding riches and great riches and unsearchable riches are all wrapped up in the beautiful expression that we call "Full Salvation." Now we read in 2 Corinthians, 8:9, where Paul said, "For ye know the grace of our Lord Jesus Christ, that though he was rich, yet for your sakes he became poor, that ye through his poverty might be rich." Again we read in Revelation 3:18 verse Christ said again to the people, "I counsel you to buy of me gold tried in the fire that ye may be rich, and white raiment that thou mayest be clothed and that the shame of thy nakedness do not appear, and anoint thine eyes with eye salve, that thou mayest see." We believe that the reader will agree with us that all these beautiful things concerning riches are found wrapped up in that wonderful expression of "unsearchable riches." For a dying saint with the angels around him with his vision so enlarged and clarified that he can look clear through into heaven is evidently in possession of something that is wonderful, it is beyond the comprehension of the finite mind. So rich, so beautiful, so glorious so eternal that God just summed it up in that wonderful expression of "unsearchable riches." Bless His name! Amen!

25

Promises

To the readers of the household of faith: What say you? Suppose you and I take two or three minutes and look at the rich things that have been promised us? Now you remember in our preceding chapter we talked about the four expressions of riches. Now we find four things in the Book that are exceedingly interesting to us. The first one is "promises," the second is "exceeding promises," the third one is "great promises," the fourth one is "precious promises." Here you will notice that we reach the climax on the fourth round. For while in our preceding chapters we reached the climax on the fourth round when we came to "unsearchable riches," also in this chapter we reach the climax on the fourth round which is "precious promises."

Everything that is included in the word salvation is brought to us under one or the other of these four promises. I suppose the people of God have rejoiced more and have gotten greater comfort and joy and satisfaction out of the promises of the Bible than out of anything else. In fact, there is more talk about the promises, and more shouting over the promises, than any other one thing in the Book. I have often heard some one quote a rich promise in the Bible and a dozen saints would leap in the air and praise God for the rich promises, and there are so many of them and so much joy and comfort to be found in them that we could not in this chapter name half of them. But we will just refer you to a few that you can take your concordance and look up at your leisure. One great promise to us is He says, "Fear thou not, for I am with thee, be not dismayed for I am thy God, I will help thee, I will uphold thee with the right hand of my righteousness." Another is, "I will never leave thee nor forsake thee, my presence will go with thee, and I will lead thee by my Spirit and I will guide thee with mine eye," and "I will cover thee with my feathers," and "You shall dwell in the land of good things," and "You shall he satisfied with the fatness of my house." "I will be a wall of fire around about thee, and the glory in the midst thereof." "Behold I have graven thee on the palms of my hands and thy walls are continually before me." "I will pour water on him that is thirsty, and floods upon the dry ground. I will pour my spirit upon thy seed and my blessing upon thine offspring, and they shall spring up as among the grass as willows by the water courses." Again the reader might shout over these beautiful promises. "Until the spirit be poured upon us from on high, and the wilderness be a fruitful field, and the fruitful field be counted for a forest, then judgment shall dwell in the wilderness, and righteousness remain in the fruitful fields, and the work of righteousness shall be peace and the effect of righteousness quietness and assurance forever. And my people shall dwell in a peaceable habitation, and in sure dwellings and in quiet resting places."

Beloved, we next notice a beautiful promise that will make your heart rejoice. "And the Lord shall guide thee continually and satisfy thy soul in drought and make fat thy bones and thou shalt be like a watered garden and like a spring of water whose waters fail not." The reader will notice that these are only a few out of the thousands of rich promises that have caused the hearts of the saints to rejoice. Thank God, there is not a promise in the Bible but what it is so large that a saint can lie down and stretch out on it, and can not kick the footboard nor scratch the headboard, nor touch the railings on either side. You can swing out over the pit of outer darkness on any promise in the old Book, and the Devil can't even throw soot on your spotless robe. Thank God for a salvation from all sin, for all men, promised through the atoning blood, of the blessed Son of God. Amen!

26

Joy

WE HAVE JUST NOTICED the four expressions of riches, and the four expressions of promises. We will now spend a few minutes talking about joy. We find joy under four different heads. The book speaks of "joy," "exceeding joy," "great joy," and "joy unspeakable and full of glory." It is the most joyful thing in the world to talk joy, and just as sure as you go to talking about joy, the "joy wagon" will drive up to your front door and the Lord will throw out a few scoop shovels of joy, and then He will hand you over a spoon and tell you to help yourself. And as you go to throwing out joy with a spoon, God will go to throwing it in with a scoop shovel, and as His measure is so much larger than yours, of course He will keep ahead of you all the time.

Well now, beloved, this last expression that the Lord calls "joy unspeakable and full of glory" is the biggest thing that a man ever saw. It is so big that it looks a good deal like a man had thrown away his spoon and jumped into the river, or the footlog broke and the man fell headforemost into a hogshead of honey and got drowned, or it makes a fellow feel like he was lying down in a hundred-acre field of red top clover, where a thousand bald-headed bumblebees had their bills in the clover blossoms, and as they look over at a fellow they just grinned and said, "Don't talk to us about the high cost of living, for we have more than we can use." Now, beloved, that is just a faint hint at "joy unspeakable and full of glory." Sometimes it comes in such waves that you want to leap up and down. At other times you want to keep quiet, at other times you want to sit down and cry, and at other times you can't keep from laughing, and then the Lord blesses your heart. Maybe the next wave that strikes you you will laugh and cry both at the same time, and you couldn't tell what you were laughing at and you never will know what you were crying about, but it is one of the manifestations of "joy unspeakable and full of glory."

27

Some Questions and Answers

HERE ARE JUST A few of the greatest questions that God has ever asked man. In studying the Book we find God asked man four questions that when they are thoroughly understood the reader will see that they cover all the ground that a sinful man has ever stood on. First, we see that God asked man this question: "Where art thou?" The second question is, "Where is thy brother?" The third question is, "What hast thou done?" The fourth question is, "What hearest thou?" These four questions will cover every condition of life that any sinner can possibly be in, and we find that the answers that man gives to God are the most fearful that ever fell from the lips of man.

First, man said, "I have sinned"; second, man said, "I was afraid"; third, man said, "I have hid myself"; fourth, man said, "I am undone." The reader will notice that these four questions and answers locate man in any condition, in any age of this old world. We find that every question God has ever asked man comes under the head of one of these four questions, and we find in these four confessions that man has made every confession that it is possible for man to make on earth.

How well I remember when I made my first confession to God, "I have sinned," but I meant it from my heart, and God listened to my confession and then said to me, "Are you willing to forsake?" and I said, "Yes, Lord, I forsake all known sin." God said, "Though thou art guilty, yet by confessing and forsaking your sins heaven is simply promised to the man that will forsake all known sin." And the Lord gave me to understand that every redeemed saint that is now in glory went over the same route that I was then traveling. But let us remember, the Book said, "He that covereth his sins, shall not prosper, but whoso confesseth and forsaketh them shall have mercy."

Then the apostle said upon another occasion, "With the heart man believeth unto righteousness and with the mouth confession is made unto salvation." May God grant that every sinner that is now on the face of the earth may draw close enough to God to hear Him say, "Where art thou?" and may he answer from the deep of his heart, "I have sinned, but I now turn my back on sin and my face toward God." This is the whole plan of salvation. There is nothing better on earth that a sinner can do than to confess and forsake and to repent of and to turn his back on sin, and nothing on earth he can do that is better than to turn his face toward God and look up through his tears and plead for mercy through the shed blood of the dying Son of God. Thank God, when I gave up all sin and set my face to go to heaven, Jesus was there to meet me, to help me over the hills and rough places of life. Praise His name forever and ever

28

My Objections to a Sinning Religion

FOR A FEW MINUTES we just want to give you a few of our objections to a sinning religion. For almost everywhere we go the good people tell us that their pastors preach to them almost every Sunday that they are sinners now and always will be while they are in the flesh and that they sin every day in word and thought and deed, and that they are just as good as anybody else and that everybody else sins just like they do and yet they never stop to think how inconsistent it is. Of course, if a man is religious and sins every day he must have a sinning religion, and a sinning religion evidently is not the kind of salvation that Jesus purchased for a lost world. We read in James 1:27, "Pure religion and undefiled before God and the Father is this, to visit the fatherless and widows in their affliction and to keep himself unspotted from the world." The reader will see here that the very fact of a pure religion denotes the fact that there are impure religions in the country. For when you hear a man say, "This is a genuine dollar," he means by that that it is not a counterfeit dollar. Of course a religion that is a pure religion would denote that many religions are counterfeit. A pure religion would denote that there are counterfeits in the country, but also a pure religion denotes that a man has been saved from all sin, and purified and made pure.

Now my next objection to a sinning religion is, first, that the atonement provides a salvation from all sin, for all men, for we read in Titus 2:11:14 verse, "For the grace of God that bringeth salvation hath appeared to all men, teaching us that denying ungodliness and worldly lusts, we should live soberly, righteously and godly in this present world, looking for that blessed hope and the glorious appearing of the great God, and our Savior Jesus Christ, who gave himself for us that he might redeem us from all iniquity and purify unto himself a peculiar people zealous of good works." Now in this quotation the author says that we were redeemed from all iniquity, and then he adds, "and purified."

Then he tells us that we are to live a life of holiness and righteousness in this present world, and not in heaven. Of course we expect to live holy in heaven, there is no dispute in that, but where the war breaks out is, some claim we can't live right in this world, and others claim we can. The man that says he can is evidently in harmony with the teachings of God's Word, and the man that says he can't is without doubt out of harmony with God and the teachings of the Book.

Then the Lord tells us also in this quotation that we are to be a peculiar people. Now, in the minds of some people, a peculiar man or woman is a person that wears a peculiar kind of a dress. In that they take a ribbon off of their hat or leave off their necktie, or cut the two little buttons off their coat sleeves, or that they eat in a certain way or certain things they don't eat. Some people believe if they don't eat pork or oysters they are peculiar and fulfilling the Scriptures. Many people imagine that if they don't wear certain things or don't eat certain things that within itself will make them peculiar people, but, according to the Book there is but one thing to that makes man peculiar, and that is to be saved from all sin and then good common-sense will regulate his eating and his wearing.

My next objection to a sinning religion is found in this fact that the least religion a man can have to have any at all will settle the sinning question. For we read in 1st John 3d chapter 9th verse, "Whosoever is born of God doth not commit sin for his seed remaineth in him and he can not sin because he is born of God." I want the reader to see that as great as the new birth is, and as far-reaching, and as eternal as it is, and as wonderful and glorious as the experience of the new birth, still it is the least experience that God gives to man. For if a sinner gets anything below the new birth, he gets nothing. However, we don't teach that the new birth is a small blessing or a little insignificant experience. It is a tremendous experience, and, sorry to say, so much bigger than the average man has nowadays, that the average man in the church when he meets a man that is really born again, often accuses the fellow of professing holiness.

My next objection to a sinning religion is found in the fact that a sinning religion would make no distinction at all between a sinner and a Christian, and there should he a distinction between them, and the lines of separation between the two should be so clearly marked that any man could detect it. Now we read in 1st John 3d chapter 8th verse, "He that committeth sin is of the devil, for the devil sinneth from the beginning." Then we read in the 9th verse, "Whosoever is born of God doth not commit sin," and then in the 10th verse, "In this the children of God are manifest and the children of the devil." Now if this means anything in the world, it means God's children don't commit sin and the Devil's children do. We have just read in the preceding verse if a man is born again, he can not commit sin, and that doesn't mean if a man professes holiness that he can't commit it. It simply means that any man that is born of the Spirit of God has been brought into such a relationship with God, that he has gone completely out of the sin business. We have often heard worldly church members say that the holiness people said they couldn't sin if they wanted to, but the Bible said that the converted man can't do it. We next notice that a sinning religion would make God swear a lie, but somebody might say, "Brother Robinson, you should not talk that way." Yes, Brother Robinson ought to be honest, and if a man can not be saved from sin God is a liar. We say not to be rude, or unmanly, but because from what we read in the Bible it is impossible for us to say anything else, for we read in Luke 1st chapter 73d, 74th, and 75th verses, "The oath which he sware to our father Abraham that he would grant unto us that we being delivered out of the hand of our enemies might serve him without fear in holiness and righteousness all the days of our lives."

Now here the reader will notice that God put Himself on oath that He would deliver us from the hands of our enemies that we might serve Him without fear in holiness and righteousness before Him all the days of our life, and beloved, all the days of a man's life are not the last days, so some men are ready to tell us that they believe in being made holy in death, but God said we are to have it all the days of our life. You will notice the two expressions, holiness and righteousness; it means that inward holiness will produce outward righteousness, and there is no better condition than that in this country—holy on the inside and righteous on the outside is God's standard, so he is clean on both sides—inside and out.

I heard the Rev. Seth C. Rees say once that, "Salvation is a revolution and not an evolution, that regeneration is a revolution that turns a man upside down, and that sanctification is a revolution that turns a man inside out." This is all brought about, as we have just noticed, through the oath that our Father sware unto us. And beloved, when our heavenly Father puts Himself on oath that we should have a thing, why should we listen to unbelievers and backsliders although they may be in the pulpit? A sinner in the pulpit is the most dangerous man in the land.

29

The Fullness of Christ

I WANT TO TALK to you a few minutes about the fullness of Christ. We read in the 1st chapter of John and at the 16th verse, these wonderful words, "And of his fullness have all we received, and grace for grace." If this text means anything, it means that every grace that budded and grew and blossomed and bore fruit in the life of Jesus Christ, we are to have a like grace in our life. It means that whatever Jesus was full of, that you are to be filled with, or whatever He was filled with, you are to be full of, and if we can find out what He was full of, then we will have no trouble in finding out what we are to be filled with. In making this discovery we will find the key that will unlock the door of the whole situation and let us into the storehouse of the fullness of Christ. Now in Col. 1st chapter 19th verse St. Paul says, "It pleased the Father that in him should all fullness dwell." In this quotation we have a hint at what we are about to receive, and so we read again in Col. 2d chapter 9th verse where the apostle says, "For in him dwelleth all the fullness of the Godhead bodily." Now this text tells us that the triune Godhead dwells in Christ. Now in connection with this text in Eph. 3d chapter 17th verse Paul says that "Christ is to dwell in our hearts by faith." Now if the Godhead dwells in Christ, and Christ dwells in us, we will understand what He means when He said, "And of his fullness have all we received." But we will make that point a little clearer or some one might say, "Does the Godhead dwell in Christ?" And we say "yes," and prove it by these two Scriptures. First, in 2 Cor. 5th chapter 19th verse we read, "To wit that God was in Christ reconciling the world unto himself." Now here is God the Father in God the Son and God the Son in humanity, and the Son in humanity is God the Father, reconciling the Father and the human family.

The next Scripture that we will use to prove that the Godhead dwells in Christ, is the third chapter of John and the 34th verse, we read that "God the Father gave not the Spirit by measure unto Jesus." That proves that Jesus Christ was so great that He could comprehend the Godhead.

But that isn't all: when we think of the fullness of Christ, the very statement means even more than we have named. For we read again in Col. 3d chapter 3d verse, "In whom are hid all the treasures of wisdom and knowledge." Then we understand what Paul meant in 1st Cor. 1st chapter and 13th verse where he said. "But of him are ye in Christ Jesus, who of God is made unto us wisdom and righteousness and sanctification and redemption." And further we read in Luke 1st chapter 15th verse where the Lord said to the disciples, "For I will give you a mouth and a wisdom which all your adversaries shall not be able to gainsay or resist."

Now we have noticed a few things at least to show what it means to us to be filled with all the fullness of Christ. Again we notice when we think of the fullness of Christ and that we are to be filled with everything that was in Him, that He was full of gentleness, and if the Book means anything, it means that we are to be gentle as He was gentle. Again we notice that He was full of patience. He never manifested a spell of impatience. He was patient with Pontius Pilate when He was on trial for His life, and He was patient when Peter drew his sword and cut off a man's ear; He was patient with James and John when they wanted to call down fire and burn up people who did not want to hear Jesus preach. So you see if we have His fullness, we will have a good supply of patience. He was also full of purity. Not an unclean word was ever uttered by the Son of God. He has been called the "Lily White" Christ and if we are full of what He was filled with, we will have in stock a large supply of purity. Christ was filled with the spirit of charity. We read that He gave His life for the world, and His clothes to His enemies, and His back to the smiters, and His cheeks to them that plucked off the hair. So if we are filled with what He was full of, we will have plenty of charity toward the other fellow.

30

The Five Crowns

BELOVED, IT MIGHT BE interesting to you to stop working and toiling long enough to just look over your estate and see what you have and what you are later on to come into possession of. First, in Jas. 1st chapter 12th verse James says "Blessed is the man that endureth temptation for when he is tried he shall receive the crown of life which the Lord has promised to them that love him." Here we see that the crown of life is won by enduring temptation. There is nothing so hard to endure as temptation, and yet nothing pays as large dividends on the investment that we make.

But we notice again in the second place that in 2 Tim. 4th chapter 6th, 7th, and 8th verses, that we are to receive another crown. Here are the words of the apostle: "For I am now ready to be offered and the time of my departure is at hand. I have fought a good fight, I have finished my course, I have kept the faith, henceforth there is laid up for me a crown of righteousness, which the Lord, the righteous judge shall give me at that day, and not to me only but unto all them also that love his appearing." Now here we see that the crown of righteousness is won by keeping the faith.

Third, we notice in 1st Thes. 2d chapter 19th verse that we are to receive another crown, and this is the "crown of rejoicing," which is the soul-winner's crown. For the apostle says, "For what is our hope, our joy, our crown of rejoicing? Are not even ye in the presence of our Lord Jesus Christ at his coming?" Now the soul-winner's crown is won by winning souls, and everybody can take part in soul-winning, and all hands should have this crown. But the average church member imagines that he is not to win souls but that the pastor is, but the reader will remember that God describes the pastor as the shepherd of the sheep, He describes the church members as the flock of sheep. We must not forget that the sheep is to produce both the lambs and the wool, and the business of the shepherd is to keep the sheep well fed and to beat back the wolves and mountain lions.

Fourth, we notice that we are to receive another crown. In 1st Peter 5th chapter 4th verse, he says, "And when the chief Shepherd shall appear, ye shall receive a crown of glory that fadeth not away." This crown St. Peter says is won by feeding the flock of God. Now many thought that nobody could receive this crown but the pastor, but that is another mistake, for let it be remembered that it will be impossible for the pastor to feed the flock as it should be fed, unless the flock in return feeds the pastor. A pastor that is well fed will make a good feeder, and if the church starves out its pastor until he has to sell goods, or plead law, or practice medicine, or run a farm to earn bread it will be impossible for him to feed them as they should be fed; therefore, both the shepherd and the flock have a chance to win a crown of glory.

Fifth, we are to receive another crown. In 1st Cor. the 9th chapter, from the 24th to 27th verse, we read these remarkable words as they fell from the lips of the great apostle, "Know ye not that they which run in a race run all, but one receiveth the prize? So run that ye may obtain and every man that striveth for the mastery is temperate in all things. Now they do it to obtain a corruptible crown, but we an incorruptible. I therefore, so run not as uncertainly, so fight I not as one that beateth the air, but I keep under my body and bring it into submission, lest that by any means when I have preached to others I myself should he a castaway." The reader will notice that the incorruptible crown is won by running this race in faith and keeping our bodies under and bringing them into subjection.

Just a word of explanation: Here is the way we receive these five crowns. The crown of life is won by enduring temptation, the crown of righteousness is won by keeping the faith; the crown of rejoicing is won by winning souls; the crown of glory is won by feeding the flock of God; and the incorruptible crown is won by keeping our bodies under and bringing them into subjection. Bless God, I am after all five of these crowns. Beloved, I want every one of them, and I ought to have them, and it is none of the Devil's business. Amen!

31

The Moth-Eaten Garment

WE WANT TO TALK with you awhile about the moth-eaten garment. I had preached many years before I gave any thought at all to the many passages of Scripture on the moth-eaten garment, and I am indebted to an old friend of mine, Dr. MacCammon, who gave me light on many of these peculiar passages concerning the moth and the moth-eaten garment. Our readers will remember that in reading the Holy Book we very frequently run across the word "moth" or "moth-eaten garment." One remarkable passage is found in Isaiah 50th chapter 9th verse, "Behold, the Lord God will help me, who is he that shall condemn me? Lo, they all shall wax old as doth a garment, the moth shall eat them up." The Bible has much to say concerning the moth, and we very frequently hear the peculiar expression "a moth-eaten garment." That expression is a very familiar one in the reading of God's Word.

We next notice in the Book of Job 4th chapter 19 verse, Job speaks of our bodies as "houses of clay which are crushed before the moth." In speaking of those that have suffered severe judgments, Job also says in the 13th chapter 28th verse, "they are as moth-eaten garments." To further illustrate man's folly in providing earthly things, or in building up his fortunes by methods of injustice, in Job 27th chapter 18th verse also he says, "He buildeth his house as a moth to set forth God's judgment against the priest and the people and the princes of Israel for their manifold sins.

We find the little Prophet Hosea comes to the platform and sets forth his warning in the 5th chapter 12th verse. Here is his peculiar statement: "Therefore will I be unto Ephraim as a moth and to the house of Judah as rottenness," but in the margin, it says, "as a worm." The Apostle James, 5th chapter 2nd verse, in threatening the rich men says, "Your riches are corrupted, and your garments are moth-eaten." This seems to unite two strange facts, corruption and moth-eaten garments. My judgment is it would be the black, dark, subtle things that are hidden in the hearts of men that crave this world more than they crave righteousness and holiness.

Now we notice that Jesus comes in at this place and refers to the little moth. If the reader will turn to that wonderful Sermon on the Mount, in the 6th chapter and 19th verse, Christ says to us, "Lay not up for yourselves treasures upon earth, where moth and rust doth corrupt and where thieves break through and steal, but lay up for yourselves treasures in heaven where neither moth nor rust doth corrupt, and where thieves do not break through nor steal" (Matt. 6:19-20). Then He adds this wonderful statement: "For where your treasure is, there will your heart be also." The reader will notice here the strange similarity between a thief and a moth. Jesus seems to put the little moth along side of the thief. I suppose that He is revealing to you the fact that the thief will come uninvited, unsolicited, and, in fact, undesired, and pilfer your home, and carry away your most valuable treasures. It would be common for a thief to carry away your best fur coat, and flannel wear and woolen blankets, and all the household goods that are so valuable. Just so with the little moth. He also will come uninvited and unsolicited, and undesired, and enter into the house without your knowledge and simply make havoc of the best things on the plantation.

The reader will remember now in our first text quoted, Isaiah 50th chapter 9th verse, the prophet there compared the wicked to moth-eaten clothes, and tells us they shall wax old as a moth-eaten garment, and that the moth will eat them up. So we see the wicked will finally be consumed and be as worthless as a moth-eaten garment. It would seem from the reading of the Bible that even in the days when the inspired men wrote the Bible God was unable to do anything with the rich men and that continues down to the present day. A rich man is worth but little more to the world, if any, than a moth-eaten garment is to its owner.

Now if we will turn to Isaiah 51st chapter 8th verse, we have in a sense the same figure used. For the old prophet says, "The moth shall eat them up like a garment, and the worm shall eat them like wool, but my righteousness shall be forever, and my salvation from generation to generation." Here the reader will notice that God makes a comparison of sin and salvation, using the moth to represent sin. For He said, "The moth shall eat them up like a garment and shall eat them like wool. But, my righteousness shall be forever, and my salvation from generation to generation."

You see there is no power in the world that can offset sin but salvation, and as truly as a moth consumes a garment, sin consumes a sinner. Some people may imagine that there would be no place to write on as small as an insect as the moth, feeling that he is not large enough to be used in illustrating sin. But as small and insignificant as a moth is, he is used throughout the Scriptures as a type of that destructive thing that we call sin. So we offer no apology to the reader for writing about this peculiar insect; in fact the moth is so powerful in its work of destruction that it might be discussed by the most brilliant minds of the nation, before the most cultured and refined and intellectual congregations of the earth.

When the prophets of old and the apostles of latter days and even our blessed Saviour himself made such frequent use of it, in all of their wonderful teachings, we see that the moth has a wonderful place in the history of our homes. Who has not seen this little white shining silver-colored insect that our text speaks about flying about in our homes at night, that creeps in so silently among the furs and flannels and other woolen stuff and gradually eats through them until a garment becomes perfectly useless and is fit only for the scrap pile, when a few days ago it was so valuable to us and such a precious garment, or a fur that was to us of almost untold value. What a picture we have here now of the destructive work of sin!

It may be interesting and profitable to us to note the striking resemblance there is between a moth and sin. Perhaps by studying this comparison closely and scripturally we may be led to see the awful effects of sin, which is so destructive to human happiness, and forsake it.

First, the moth is a little, insignificant insect, and its smallness is quite apparent, but that very smallness makes it no less destructive.

The smallness of this little insect is absolutely in its favor, and very much against us and to our great disadvantage. If it were very large it would be no trouble to either see it or hear it as it made its approach. But how small it is, and how silently it makes its way into the best wardrobe, and what fearful destruction it makes of the winter clothing, and its deadly work is always on the best garments. It is even so with sin. To so many people Adam's sin was so small that it did not amount to anything, and yet see how it has affected the whole human race. It has made the earth to heave and groan. It has robbed heaven of millions of its brightest ornaments and has also built our great state prisons, which are in a sense our hells on earth. For our state prisons are places of banishment and punishment, and sin has filled them with precious human souls, and has kindled its fires of sin and vice and degradation, and has finally populated hell with precious souls, where "the smoke of their torment ascends upward for ever and ever."

The Devil has tried to make you believe, no doubt, that the thing you have committed is so small it doesn't amount to anything, or will never harm you, but just stop and think a moment of that one sin of Adam. Think of the wrecked homes, broken hearts, ruined lives, blighted prospects; think of the wails, moans, and groans of the offspring of Adam; and all of this misery and wretchedness was brought about by only one sin.

Here is a plain, practical illustration that will illustrate this one little sin. Think of this, just one little leak in the vessel will sink the whole ship and drown everyone that is on board. The vessel doesn't have to have a thousand leaks in it. Let it spring one leak, and that leak be allowed to remain there unchecked and unstopped and it isn't long until that great vessel is lying on the bottom of the sea. So these so-called little sins may prove just as destructive to the soul as the leak did to the vessel. Here is another point that I want to notice. A pin wound may destroy the life of the most useful man in the nation and prove as fatal as a rifle ball. A pistol will kill as surely as a cannon. A penknife will open the vein and let out the life's blood just as easily as a sword. You had better be on the lookout for that little moth that will enter the home and destroy the best garment in the building;

and just so you had better be on the lookout for that little sin that may enter in without notice and destroy both soul and body in hell.

It was a very small thing when the cow of Mrs. O'Leary kicked over that little kerosene lamp, but it started a fire that in forty-eight hours had swept over a strip of Chicago four miles long and one mile wide, destroyed 17,450 homes and millions of dollars' worth of property, and left multiplied thousands of people homeless. The Apostle James says, "Behold, how great a matter a little fire kindleth!" See James 3:5, and that will give you some light on the fearfulness of the Chicago disaster. The first wrong act of your life may seem to you to be a very small thing, but, beloved, it may cost you your soul; and others may be influenced by your act and so it may mean their destruction also.

We next notice that the moth works noiselessly and secretly. If it came into our house with some great demonstration, or would herald its approach by the bugle sound, we might be on our guard, but instead it steals in secretly and unperceived and proceeds with its destructive work. It is even so with sin.

What an awful destruction it has worked in a secret way. I read a little story one day of some shepherds who were watching their flocks and they discovered an eagle and watched it soar from the crag. It flew majestically far up into the sky, but by and by it became unsteady in its motions and began to waver in its flight. At length one wing drooped and then the other. The poor bird struggled vainly for a moment and then fell swiftly to the ground. The shepherds sought the fallen bird to see what was the cause of that fearful fall from such heights in the blue sky and, behold, they found a little serpent had fastened itself upon this eagle while it rested upon the crag. The eagle did not know the serpent was there, but the dangerous little reptile had fastened himself upon that game bird, and gnawed through the feathers; and while the proud monarch was sweeping through the air, the serpent's fangs were thrust into the flesh, and the eagle came reeling down into the dust. This illustrates the story of many human lives. How many of the most brilliant minds we have seen start out with such splendid promise and it seemed they were going to soar to the heights of fame and honor; when they would finally begin to stagger and reel and fight and struggle, and eagle-like they would finally fall! The fact is, some secret sin like the little moth, had crept in almost unawares, eating its way to the heart, and at last the proud life lies soiled and dishonored in the dust. We need to be ever on the watch against these treacherous and insidious perils, these little secret sins which, unperceived, work death to the soul.

We next notice that the moth works from the inside out. It will creep in among the woolen garments and there will lay its eggs which after a little while will hatch out and the little worms are there in the warp and woof of the cloth and they feed upon its fiber. Or to make it still plainer, they draw their life from the life of the cloth, and in a short time there is no life left in the cloth, it lies before you now, a moth-eaten garment. How much like the hidden sin in the heart and life of man. It is not long until this little worm changes into the regular moth, but by the time it chrysalizes and emerges into the full-grown moth, the garment is completely spoiled and wrecked and useless to man. What a life-size picture of sin is this!

As truly as the moth will destroy the beautiful garment, so sin will destroy the most beautiful life, and sin, like the moth, begins on the inside and works toward the outside. Sin can do no harm until it finds a lodging in the heart. Now you will remember the words of Jesus and St. Paul when they both spoke of that deadly thing we call sin. Jesus said, "For out of the heart proceed evil thoughts." And then He gave that fearful picture in the 7th chapter of St. Mark's Gospel. But all of those fearful things that He spoke of, He says are just the outcroppings of sin in the inward life. If you will let sin get once lodged in the heart, it will eat its way to the outward life. Did you ever think that Satan could do nothing with our first parents until he gained access to their hearts by means of an outward sin? Once the hearts were entered, disobedience soon followed. Seeing therefore how important it is to guard this little channel to the heart the wise man said, "Keep thy heart with all diligence, for out of it are the issues of life" (Prov. 4:23). He also said in Proverbs 23d chapter 7th verse, "As he thinketh in his heart, so is he."

We next notice that the moth works the greatest havoc on garments that are not in use. It is the furs and flannels and woolen garments that are put away in the summer time awaiting the return of the winter that suffer the most from the ravages of the moth. The garments that we wear every day don't seem to attract him. This is also true in regard to sin. Sin seems to make but little or no inroads into that soul that is busy working for Jesus with the love of God shed abroad in his heart and his life hid with Christ in God. But just think of that idle soul that is always a party to sin. The statement "Will it remain forever true, that Satan finds some mischief still for idle hands to do." It has often been said that "An idle brain is the devil's workshop."

I have noticed that a young man or woman with nothing to do but lie around town or loafing on the street corners, wasting time, soon becomes vicious and sinful, unmanly, and unwomanly. The most of the dark, black, murky, muddy, mysterious, unbelievable, unthinkable, and unknowable schemes that have been pulled off in the last quarter of a century, ninety-nine out of a hundred of them have been planned by a crop of idlers and street loafers, so it still remains true that our idle days are Satan's busy days. Idleness is simply an inlet to temptation, but the Christian who is busy in the Master's service, trying to rescue the perishing and lifting up the fallen, cheering the sad-hearted, strengthening the weak, and comforting the lonely, won't be troubled much with sin's alluring bait.

Next, the moth is no respecter of persons; it spares neither the rich nor the poor, the high nor the low, the learned nor ignorant, the black or white, red, brown or yellow, the philosopher nor the fool. It exempts no one from its work of destruction. The rich with their expensive furs and costly woolen wear, and the poor with their cheaper and coarser wear are alike subject to its attacks. This is also true of sin. It is everywhere doing its hellish work of destruction among the children of men. Go into our jails or penitentiaries and you will see there the classes that have been touched by sin. There you will see men of wealth, businessmen, senators, congressmen, lawyers, doctors, preachers, and great statesmen, men of talent, culture, and refinement, but through sin their lives have been blackened and there they are dragging out an existence with soiled and dishonored names, and behind prison bars.

These men with such wonderful opportunities before them probably had imagined that the little sins they first committed could never destroy them. Oh, they had seen others who had been wrecked but they said that with their brilliant minds, wealth, and social standing sin could never put them down, but just as truly as the little moth has destroyed the best garments in the home, sin has destroyed the brightest minds of our nation. As the moth eats the fiber and destroys the garments, so sin has worked its deadly fangs into their very heart and life, and now they are dying by the inch and their names are a hiss and a byword where they used to be honored and respected by everyone.

We next notice some of the remedies for the cure of this little insect we call the moth. It is needless to say that the remedies are many and of various kinds. Some ladies have used the red cedar chest, others have packed their clothes in newspapers, believing that the moth won't bother clothes that are packed, thinking that a moth can't live where printer's ink is found. Others have used tobacco, they say, with good effect. Still others have used the mothballs, but the smell of the mothball was almost as bad as the moths themselves, and the smell of tobacco was worse. Others have used what they call "tar paper," but the yellow spot was so hard to get off the blankets that at last they had to abandon even the tar paper; for after several years of hot water and good soap the yellow tar spots were still there. We have heard of many other remedies. I suppose there have been scores and scores of remedies used to try to dislocate and drive out and destroy this troublesome little insect that we call the moth. But after all the remedies that man can conceive of and after all the remedies that women have applied to destroy the moth, we still have this deadly little insect. Its deadly work is still going on in its destruction of the garments of the poor people of the earth.

So it is today with men and sin. For all the past ages men have been trying the various remedies for sin and, like the remedies for the moth, they so far have all failed. One remedy for sin men have told us was for us to put up a stiff fight against the inclinations to wrongdoing and by so doing we would get rid of the thing, and that we by putting up a stiff fight would come off more than conquerors. Others have said that all we need to get rid of sin is to be well born, well fed, and well educated, and to rise up in our own power and make a man of yourself and down the sin.

We heard of a father who had a son that was given to taking things that didn't belong to him, and of course the father wanted to cure the son of the awful disease of sin, so the old man tied the boy's hands behind him in order to cure him of theft. Another fellow was always getting drunk and the city authorities said that he had to be cured of drunkenness and so they locked him up in jail. By so doing they hoped to cure him of the drink habit, believing that the jail was the remedy for drunkenness. The father that tied the boy's hands to cure him of stealing did not seem to realize that the poor boy had stolen these goods with his heart and not with his hands, for back behind the hands was the boy's will power, and back behind the will power was that dark, black, muddy, murky, mysterious, unbelievable, un-thinkable, unexplainable something that the scientists call heredity and that the theologians call depravity, that the Bible calls carnality.

When two poor old sinners get drunk and have a fight and are arrested and brought to trial, and pay out as much for a fine as they will make in a month of hard labor, when they undertake to explain the thing they call it deviltry, and this is the thing that causes a man to get drunk or to steal. For who has not seen men by the hundred who really wanted to do right and did their best to use their will power but that peculiar thing that we call the carnal self was so uncontrolled that the poor man would go down in spite of his will power. So it is something away back in the man's life that must be touched by di-vinity, and lifted out and removed before the poor man can be set right and even do what he feels that he ought to do.

I have known preachers who rejected holiness and the second work of grace and called holiness people "second-blessingists" and yet in their own pulpits in trying to make the people do right and come across and do good I have known them to even lose their temper and almost go into a rage, and at the same time before they would leave the pulpit deny the remedy for worldliness in the heart of a be-liever. For as long as carnality is there, the man is going with the world, and the only hope in the world to get the world out of a man is to get him sanctified wholly and filled with the Holy Ghost.

The man who is filled with the Holy Ghost will not have to be put in jail to keep him from getting drunk, and the man filled with the Holy Ghost will not have to have his hands tied to keep him from stealing. The only hope of the drunkard or the thief is first in the birth of the Spirit, and second in the baptism with the Holy Ghost and fire. This is the only remedy. This will make an honest man out of a rascal and a sober man out of a drunkard. The nature of man must be cleansed and purified. I suppose that the physician would call it constitutional treatment; that is, the remedy must go deeper than the surface. Men have tried to improve themselves by what they call "good resolutions," by "turning over a new leaf," by "rising up" as they call it, and "asserting their manhood." Though a man may be ever so sorry that he got drunk and went to jail, he may feel keenly his disgrace, and may feel he has brought a dark shadow over his home, his wife, and little ones, but as long as carnality remains in his heart he is liable to go on a drunk at almost any time. Being ashamed of the fact that he got drunk never removes the desire for strong drink.

We have known a man to take the chills and fever, as they used to call it, and take medicine and break up the chills, and for some two or three weeks he would apparently go on without any chills at all. But you could tell by looking at the man that he still had malaria in his system, and as long as that fearful disease was there, any little change in the weather would cause the chills to return and often much harder that at the beginning.

What the man really needs is to be treated, not for the chills, but for the fearful disease we call malaria, and given constitutional treatment and have the poison removed from his system, and the chills and fever will never return. And it is just so with sin. As long as sin is left in the system, anything that may take place or anything that happens; I have often known a cold snap or too much heat, or for the dry weather to hold on too long, or for the rain to come at the time when the fellow wasn't looking for it, actually caused the "Old Man" to get up in a man and cause him to have a spell and grit his teeth and pull his hair. One week he swears the dry weather is going to ruin his crop, the next week he swears the rain is ruining it.

I remember a brother of mine once. As he and I were walking through the corn field, the corn was needing rain, and he said if it didn't rain in a week he would make ten bushels of corn to the acre, but we walked on and he growled and complained of the dry weather. By the time he got to the middle of the field he said emphatically if it didn't rain in three days he wouldn't make five bushels of corn to the acre. By the time we got to the back side of the field he was gritting his teeth and pulling his hair and swearing violently and almost cursing God, and he declared that if it didn't rain in fifteen minutes he wouldn't make seed corn. Anybody can see that that was the fruits of carnality.

Just as many have thought that to jail a man would cure him of drunkenness or to tie his hands would cure him of theft, others have thought that the trouble could be removed by what they call "growing in the different graces." They call it "growing in the graces and developing the good that is in man." In fact, they claim he always had a spark of divinity in him, and that all that is needed is to fan it a little and he would finally bloom out into a walking saint by trying to develop the good that is in him and trying to hold down the bad that is in him. We have all found out that growing carnality out of the heart is never God's plan.

It has been declared by men who are in authority that there is no way to cultivate a thistle and transform it into a rose. In fact, the more you cultivate a thistle, the larger it grows, the more seed it produces, the more dangerous it becomes, and the more fearful it looks. Growing will never change the character of the thistle. Neither will it change the character of anything else. The more the hog is cultivated and the larger he grows, the more hog you have got. You cannot cultivate the goat and change him into a sheep. A big goat is as far from being a sheep as a little goat. To talk about transforming sinners into Christians by good behavior is one of the impossibilities of life, and the longer a sinner grows in sin, the more sinful he becomes. The only way that a sinner can grow in grace is to grow in disgrace. Development won't change the human heart, and there is no use in talking about growing in grace anyway until we get *into* grace. You can't ride on a train until you get aboard the train. You can't swim in water until you get into the water. This makes me feel that much that is being done nowadays to improve the human family is mere child's play. But God's plan is to strike at the very root of the matter, and through the precious blood of Christ, our Heavenly Father has made provisions whereby we can be cleansed from all sin.

But someone may say, "Don't we get rid of sin when we are converted?" If they mean the sins we have committed, we answer, "Yes," but if they mean the innate, inborn, inbred depravity that caused us to commit sin, we answer, "No." For the Book said, "Ye are babes in Christ, and yet carnal." We must not forget that there lies in the human breast, something farther back than the sins which we have committed. God has not only planned to get rid of our wrong doing, but God's method is to straighten up our wrong being, because there is something within man that cannot be forgiven, but must be cleansed.

I might give you a plain, practical illustration that came under my own observation. A mother told her little boy one day that the hall had been freshly painted, and he must not get against the wall or he would get paint all over himself. He promised faithfully he would not. So the mother went about her work, and a few hours later she found that the boy had paint all over his clothes. There was a falsehood in the boy and an act of disobedience. Now we all know the mother could forgive her boy for the falsehood and for the disobedience, and she did lovingly, and yet the paint was all over his clothes. So the boy had to have forgiveness for the thing he had done that was wrong, and then the clothes had to be cleansed. The pardon he received did not remove the paint from his clothes, that was another work of grace.

Thank God, He will forgive our sins, blot them out of His book of remembrance, and remember them against us no more forever! But bless His name, He will also go farther back and deeper down than pardon! He will go back to the root of the matter and slay the root and seed of inbred sin. This is the only sure cure for that moth that we have been telling you about. The carnal mind doesn't have to be held down like a "jack-in-the-box," and when we move the latch he will jump out every time. But if the thing is killed so dead that the life is taken out of it, that little moth of sin will never ruin another spiritual garment.

This destruction of sin must take place in this world, for we read that "there is nothing unholy or unclean or that defileth or maketh a lie or worketh abomination can enter into heaven." Remember how Jesus said, "Lay up for yourselves treasures in heaven, where neither moth nor rust doth corrupt, nor where thieves break through and steal, for where your treasure is, there will your heart be also." Thank the Lord, there is no moth in heaven. The climate is so pure that moths cannot enter there, and I can. Amen! For such a climate and for such a country and for such a home, "blessed be the Lord God, and Father of our Lord Jesus Christ, who hath blessed us with all spiritual blessings, and made us to sit together in heavenly places with Christ Jesus" [*sic*.]. Amen!

32

Barnabas, the Evangelist

OUR TEXT IS IN Acts 11:24. We read, "For he was a good man, and full of the Holy Ghost and faith and much people was added unto the Lord." This within itself is a wonderful history of a man, however in few words, yet words enough to tell us of his goodness and graces.

First, a good man; second, a man full of the Holy Ghost; third, a man full of faith; fourth, and much people added to the Lord. Now here is history enough for a large book. First, we will say concerning the early life of Barnabas, the Bible gives us but little or, we might say, no information, for it tells us nothing about his birth and nothing about his boyhood days, not a word about his education and his ancestors. In all these points the sacred record is absolutely silent. We are introduced to him at once as a full grown man with a fully developed moral manhood. We are told in Acts 4th chapter 36th verse that his first name was Joses and that he was surnamed by the apostles, Barnabas, which is, being interpreted, "the son of consolation," and that he was a Levite and of the country of Cyprus. Scant as is our knowledge of the boy, there is enough said of the man Barnabas to indicate that he was a most noble character.

His name is first mentioned in connection with a great revival of religion, which was held in Jerusalem by Peter and John. We read that Peter and John had healed the lame man at the beautiful gate of the temple and their imprisonment soon followed. Before the council that met in Jerusalem they manifested such holy boldness that the council marveled, but commanded them not to speak or teach any more in the name of Jesus. But being let go the apostles went to their own company, and reported what had been said to them. This brought the whole church together for prayers, and while they prayed, the place was shaken where they were assembled. Thank the Lord, prayer has shaken more things loose than earthquakes. This was a Holy Ghost revival, for we read that the multitudes that believed, were of one heart and one soul, and among this multitude was the young man that we call Barnabas. As we shall readily see, a revival that was so far-reaching that it unstopped deaf ears, that it opened eyes, and made the world, the flesh, and the Devil sit up and take notice, was indeed a very remarkable revival. For any revival that would bring into view and into such publicity such a man as this man Barnabas, must have been an unusual revival. At least it was no ordinary affair, and it is wonderful how a revival of Holy Ghost religion brings men into view.

How different we sometimes think of the revival of our days. They are called "modern revivals," some of them are called "decision days," others have put on what they call "drives for members," and little cards have been published and committees in the different classes of the church have gone out and walked the streets, they have button-holed men in the banks and in the post office, in grocery stores, dry goods houses, on street cars and in fact on the street corners, have presented them with a card, and kindly asked them to write their names on them, and by so doing, were to become a member of some ecclesiastical body. That is called on in our day a "drive for members." The only thing you can say for such proceedings is that a few names were added to the church roll, and we were in one city where the people that had given their names on cards were not even in the church when their names were read out. We might say now, "Oh, for an old-fashioned revival of heart-felt, old-fashioned religion that would give to the world another Barnabas," whose name shall go down in history to be perpetuated as long as the ages, and remembered by the church universal for his noble character.

We notice at this point the spirit displayed by Barnabas in those early days of the Church, that none of the believers might lack for anything. Those that had lands or houses sold them and distribution was made unto every man according as he had need. This was not a compulsory abandonment of property, but as there was only one heart and one soul among them, those who were able sold as much of their possessions as was required to provide for the needs of their poorer brothers. Charity was the rule and not the exception. Money was given for charity freely when the heart was given fully to the Lord. That early church had consecrated its purse and so we read that Barnabas, having land, sold it and brought the money and laid it at the apostle's feet. (See Acts 4th chapter 37th verse.) What a princely benefactor he was! Either the amount of his giving was very large or there was something in his manner of giving that caused Luke to single Barnabas out from all the others and only mention his name in connection with the general law of self-denying generosity. The point is that a deep inward principle of love will always find some outward expression toward those who are in need. Selfishness will think only of our own comfort, but a heart warmed by the love of Christ will always think of the general good. Barnabas did not wait for others to act, neither did he wish to outdo some one else in the matter of giving, but he gave when the needs of the people demanded it.

True liberality is both a cause and effect of every true revival. "Is his purse consecrated?" was frequently a question of one of John Wesley's co-laborers, when he heard of a man who had become a Christian. A genuine revival of old-time, heart-felt religion in the church would cause the boards of foreign missions, of the different denominations to not be smothered to death with debt, and missionaries from having their salaries cut to the point where they have to eke out an existence while they do the work of the church in the foreign fields, while the homeland has plenty and to spare. Such a revival would cause the local church to do away with all its entertainments and its festivities in order to meet the current expenses.

Not only did Barnabas assist in improving the outward and material conditions of the early church, but we see what he did to preserve the internal peace and prosperity of the church. Knowing how injurious to their peace and happiness and how destructive of the church would be any division that might spring up, we find that Barnabas became one of the peacemakers of the early church, for we read that when Paul returned to Jerusalem after his conversion on the way to Damascus many suspicioned him, for we are told in Acts 9th chapter 26th verse that "he assayed to join himself to the disciples," but they were all afraid of him, and believed not that he was a disciple. But no one could blame them, for he had been breathing out threatenings and slaughter against them, and they knew it. Here was this same man wanting to join them. Of course they thought that trouble was in the air and it was at this critical moment that Barnabas came in to calm the troubled waters. Luke tells us in Acts 9th chapter 27th verse, "Barnabas took him and brought him to the apostles, and declared unto them how he had seen the Lord in the way and that he had spoken to him[...] of the Master in the name of the Lord." This settled the whole matter, and resulted in complete confidence among the brethren. The Church thus united went on to achieve further conquest for God and righteousness.

Distinctions in any church block the way to its success. But that people will differ in their opinions of one another is to be expected, and that gossipers and mischief-makers will always exist in the community, and that religious disputes will arise from time to time can not be avoided. But the church that would thrive and flourish in revivals must be one in Spirit and co-operation. So thought Barnabas, and the methods that he employed to secure this oneness was not so much by open attack as by sympathy and persuasion. In this respect Barnabas became an example to the modern church worker.

In the church there is not so much to be gained by openly and bitterly attacking Christian Science, or Russellism or theocracy or Mormonism or, in fact, any other "ism" that is floating about the country that we have to behold everywhere we go. To say that we are to believe in and accept these heresies is, of course, untrue. In fact, we have no respect on earth for any of the above "isms" or heresies and believe them to be the offspring of the Enemy of all righteousness. But probably a much better way is to show the world that we have something much better than these "isms," and by a genial warmth of spiritual religion melt down the prejudice which stands in the way of the triumph of our holy religion.

Another thing about Barnabas we want to notice is this: He was a man that was big enough to appreciate what others had done. For when he saw the good that others had done and saw the downright goodness in other people or saw a great revival that had just been held by another evangelist, instead of Barnabas throwing any mud or sneers at the other evangelist, he could simply rejoice and his soul was filled with real happiness. For we read that "When the news reached Jerusalem that the gospel was having great success in Antioch, Barnabas was at once selected by the church to go on this mission of inquiry and encouragement." So we read in Acts 11:23, "When he came and had seen the grace of God, he was glad." Some one has said that it was a great window in the character of this beautiful man that we call Barnabas. That when he saw the great revival that was going on at Antioch, and that multitudes of people were being converted, it made him glad and he rejoiced with joy unspeakable and full of glory.

We don't read that Barnabas, when he saw the work that was done, tried to throw a wet blanket over it and look on with a kind of superior critical eye and give them to understand that if he had done the preaching the work would have been much deeper and more thorough under his preaching than what he could see had been done there. No, thank the Lord, Barnabas didn't do that, but we read that he joined in with them in the happiest and most beautiful spirit, and exhorted them all that with purpose of heart they should cleave unto the Lord Jesus Christ. In this Barnabas was different from many men that we meet. Sorry to say, some good men, it seems, can never detect goodness in other people. And because they did not have a hand in the revival themselves, they are most reluctant to give the credit to others. Thank the Lord, it was not so with Barnabas. Something must be radically wrong when such a disposition is manifested. A good man longs to see people converted any time, and under the preaching of anybody, and anywhere on the face of the earth. For we all admit that a good man hates wickedness because it grieves God and hurts men and when he finds good being done, no matter who is doing it, or who is going to get the credit for it, he rejoices. Surely anything that will make the angels in heaven rejoice ought to make good people happy down here.

Again, we notice further that Barnabas was kind and gracious and entirely free from any disposition to push himself to the front. So true was this that you will notice he was called "the son of consolation," or "the son of exhortation." I believe some one has said that this same word is used for the one and for the other. For from this word we can judge somewhat of the character of this man's preaching. It was running over with comfort. His sermons were tender and consoling and stimulating, rather than convincing. He aimed to reach the heart rather than the head. He was probably not what you would call a great preacher. He did not possess the commanding gift of St. Peter, or the splendid eloquence of the young Apollos. Neither did he possess the logical reasoning of St. Paul, but he knew the way to men's hearts, and this is a most necessary qualification in a minister's life.

In these awful days when people are being fairly crushed with the cares and burdens of life and hearts are bleeding with sorrow, and the whole world is groaning because of sin, what we need in our pulpits is not a rehash of the daily papers. We know that information such as is gathered by the great news companies has a place in the world, but what we need in our pulpits is a message of love and tenderness and comfort that will cheer and encourage the people in the struggle of life. We need to be like Barnabas, the son of consolation, not necessarily great preachers are always needed, but tender and loving, and with all, we ought to be so modest as to our own gifts as preachers as to say of others that "he must increase but I must decrease." Such a preacher was this beautiful man that the old Book calls Barnabas. When he was at Antioch and saw the great opportunities in that popular city for a great work, and having a modest approval of himself or his ability to carry on that work, he went, as we learn in Acts 11th chapter 25th and 26th verses, to Tarshish to seek out Saul, and when he found him he brought him to Antioch. He now puts Paul in the foreground. This is always the mark of a noble soul. Some men don't like it when others come in who outshine them in point of popularity, but it made no difference with Barnabas. He remained the same beautiful, humble Christlike spirit, and he was willing to keep out of sight and to bring others into the spotlight, if only the cause of righteousness might be advanced, and Christ magnified among men. Barnabas breathed the same spirit as is seen in a little poem touching the first sermon delivered by Professor Elmslie, of London, England, that noble Scotchman that went to his reward a few years ago. Here is the poem as we find it and the little history in connection with its publication:

He was to preach his first sermon in the parish of Rayne. His mother was anxious to hear her boy preach for the first time, but being unable to attend, she wrote to a friend to hear him, and to tell her frankly how the boy did. The answer was returned but was never heard of by him until a few days before his death. His sister, finding it among his mother's papers, read it to him. It was this:

He held the lamp of truth that day
  So low that none could miss the way;
And yet so high to bring in sight,
  That picture fair—the world's great light.
That gazing up the lamp between
  The hand that held it scarce was seen.

He held the pitcher, stooping low,
  To lips of little ones below.
Then raised it to the weary saint,
  And bade him drink when sick and faint.
They drank the pitcher thus between
  The hand that held it scarce was seen.

He blew the trumpet soft and clear,
  That trembling sinners need not fear.
And then with louder note, and bold
  To raze the walls of Satan's hold,
The trumpet coming thus between
  The hand that held it scarce was seen.

But when the Captain says, "Well done,
  Thou good and faithful servant, come,"
Lay down the pitcher and the lamp,
  Lay down the trumpet, leave the camp,
The weary hand will then be seen
  Clasped in those pierced ones—naught between.

From what has already been said about this splendid man, Barnabas, you will not be surprised to learn that a man of such excellent gifts would enter upon this work by a divine appointment. For we next notice in Acts 13th chapter 2d verse, where it is said, "As they ministered unto the Lord and fasted, the Holy Ghost said, Separate me Barnabas and Saul for the work whereunto I have called them." You will notice that the Holy Ghost named His men. He is very particular about the kind of men He employs, to do His work. The early church did not think so, and therefore to fill the gap caused by the fall of Judas, they proceeded to make the appointment. They selected two men, Barnabas, whose surname was Justus, and Matthias, and then the church said to the Lord, "Show which of these two men thou hast chosen, that he may take part of this apostleship from which Judas by transgression fell; and they gave forth their lots and the lot fell upon Matthias, and he was numbered with the eleven apostles." Then I will add a bit that is not in the old Book. For after the apostles gave forth their lots and it fell upon Matthias, and he was numbered with the eleven apostles, we never hear of him again.

The fact is that of the two men that the apostles set before the Lord and asked Him which of the two men he had chosen to take part of the apostleship that was lost in the fall of Judas, the Lord had not chosen either one of them. No doubt but what either of them were most excellent men, and beautiful Christian gentlemen, and are today, I think, both in heaven, but the man that our gracious heavenly Father had in mind to fill the vacancy that was made by the fall of Judas was none other than a little Hebrew, that we call "Saul of Tarsus." Everything goes to prove that fact. It was simply a mistake the apostles made, and instead of waiting on the Lord to give the Holy Ghost a chance to appoint a man to take the place of Judas, they took the whole matter into their own hands, for evidently the Lord did not want either of the two men that were nominated by the apostles.

Nothing is left to a mere haphazard way in God's choice in His call of men to do the work of His kingdom. We see it made perfectly plain here when the blessed Holy Ghost said, "Separate me Barnabas and Saul for the work whereunto I have called them." This leads me to say that God's choice of men is not determined so much by their intellectual qualifications, as by their spiritual equipment. In our day we find that scholarship, culture, and great intellectual powers are being very largely set aside by the Lord. It is not because God does not demand great intellectual power and could not use a man with the greatest brain. The trouble is, when the average man spends more time in a university than he spends with his people, and packs his head with human learning, he is more or less liable to carry an empty heart. Intellectually he is above his people and spiritually he is below them. Therefore, God in self-defense and in protecting His kingdom, looks more to a man's spiritual qualification than his intellectual gifts. We know that God can use the greatest thinkers in the world if He could get them to go down in consecration and get the old man crucified and the "body of sin" destroyed and the heart filled with perfect love, and then with a burning desire to glorify God and bless the world an intellectual man, you see, could be used to better advantage than an illiterate man.

Where we find a man with a great mind and a great soul, God can get greater usefulness out of that man than He could out of the life of a man that was deeply spiritual and yet untrained intellectually. It is not in the fact that God ever sets His approval upon ignorance. That is not the thought, but God must have spiritual men to do the work of the kingdom. We have seen God use the ripest scholarship with the greatest natural gifts, and some men with the greatest brain power have been the most spiritual men of the ages, but there are not many of that class. We will take the case of Paul and Peter. They were both deeply spiritual, they were both splendid commanders, but Paul had the advantage of Peter intellectually, therefore he was used of the Lord to write more books than any other man had ever written of sacred history.

But it matters not how intellectual a man is, if the Spirit of the Lord is not in him, the Lord can not use him for spiritual work. Barnabas was evidently a God-called and a Spirit-filled man, for no man can read of Barnabas without seeing that God's seal was upon him and upon his ministry, for in Acts 11th chapter 24th verse, Luke said emphatically, "He was a good man and full of faith, and of the Holy Ghost, and much people was added to the Lord." The most beautiful thought to my mind is brought out in this most remarkable statement by the divine writer, that Barnabas was a good man. Goodness is a most precious possession, and it has been discovered that goodness will carry an apology for almost every defect that we may have, but we are told by Bible translators that the word good means more than merely morally good. It means that Barnabas was kind, affectionate, and attractive. Indeed, the commentators tell us that the word may be construed with equal propriety that Barnabas was a beautiful man. He was good or he was beautiful, just as you like it; in fact, in the kingdom of God goodness and beauty are one and the same thing.

Barnabas was so sweetly transparent that his goodness shone through his face. I mean by that his soul was so great and so beautiful and so transparent, that in looking at Barnabas you could tell at a glance that he was no ordinary human being. No doubt at one time Barnabas looked like other unsaved men, and the reader will remember that both sin and grace put their marks on a man. But thank God when we receive the Holy Ghost and the gift of righteousness, the mark of sin is so blotted out, and the mark of grace takes its place, that you can scarcely look on a Christian and imagine that he ever was a sinner. There is something about the grace of God that will illuminate from within. It was just so with Barnabas. His face took on a smile and a heavenly glow that could not be rubbed off, and it won't wear off; the longer it wears the brighter it shines. There is nothing that will improve a man's looks like a good case of old-fashioned, heart-felt, Holy Ghost religion.

I have seen people that it seemed there was a divine light somewhere within them, it seemed to shine out from their eyes and face, it would simply leak out in a handshake or a kind word. We have seen some people that had what we call some natural beauty, but they had to kind of supplement it with the various chalk and powders and perfumes that are put up by the druggist, while we see some people that apparently Nature has overlooked as far as beauty is concerned, yet they were so filled with the blessed Holy Spirit, that they were beautiful to look upon, and you could apparently look through them and see God behind them. Moses had this wonderful illumination when he came down from the mountain. His people said, "Put a veil on him or we can not look at him," and the beauty of it all is we read that Moses, "wist not that the skin of his face shone."

Some time ago we read a little story of an infidel, a Swiss artist, who was sent to make a character sketch of a Salvation Army meeting in England, but when he critically watched their faces and saw that humble band of Christian workers and the joy and peace that they enjoyed to which his own soul was a complete stranger, he was completely overcome, for as he saw the visions of the heavenly light in their faces and saw his own fearful and wretched condition, he never got away from their faces, but the vision tarried with him, until in a short time he knelt at their altar, and turning his own hard, critical face heavenward and the Salvation Army lassies knelt around him and their faces all heavenly lit, and as he wept and prayed with them for the mercy and love of God, finally the visions that were on their faces seemed to break out in his, until he arose and declared publicly that he had come to criticize, but was going away to rejoice.

Such was this man Barnabas. His goodness was not like the morning dew, it did not pass off with the rising of the sun, but during the long, sultry days the shine wore on instead of wearing off, for his heart and life were consecrated to God, which is the only guaranty for permanent integrity and righteousness. Barnabas could stand erect and unmoved in the storms of opposition and persecution, because his goodness was riveted down like a lighthouse built on a storm-swept ledge in the bed rock of a full salvation.

Another beautiful characteristic of Barnabas was, he was full of faith. This, as you will see, is saying that he was a strong, healthy believer. Faith was not only the root principle, but the mainspring and passion of his life. We heard somebody say once that there were three kinds of believers. There are half-believers, make-believers, and whole believers. Well, amen! Barnabas belongs to the latter class. Nothing was lacking in his faith, having rested alone on Christ for his salvation, and having felt His power in his own soul, he believed, beyond doubt, that the truth which he had embraced and the cause which he had espoused were of God. He was actually full of faith, and this will account for the fact that Barnabas was such a force in the early Christian Church. How refreshing in these times of religious doubt and wavering, to get near a man with so much heaven in his compassion, and one who manifests such a rich fullness of faith. The men of this character are the men that have accomplished so much for God and the Church all down the years of by-gone history.

We know that great learning and much wealth have had a wonderful place in the Church, but the men that have moved the world toward God were men of faith, often without wealth or very much learning. Some have said that faith was the mainspring of life, that without it not only the Church would die, but all business would cease as soon as faith was gone. We have reached the day and age in our time where we need a faith that will help us to lift this poor old sin-stained, heart-broken world up to God and holiness. We know that a weak, timid, vacillating faith will get us nowhere. It never has and never will, and the Lord is never pleased with such a faith, neither is the man that tries to use it. We have often heard Brother Will Huff say that God never was guilty of sending out a man to try to do something; that the man that God sent could do the thing that God sent him to do. We have often heard him say that the reason St. Paul was such a factor in the world's history was that from the time he met Jesus on the Damascus road until the day his head was chopped off by Nero he stood like he had rock ribs under his feet. The reader will remember that God said to Paul, "Fear not Paul, as thou hast borne witness in Jerusalem, so also shalt thou bear witness in Rome."

We next notice that Barnabas was full of the Holy Ghost. This is an interesting statement from the fact that so many good people believe it to be impossible to be filled with the Holy Ghost, and still others have such extravagant notions about such experience that they suppose a Spirit-filled man must be about ready to "sprout wings," as they often call it, and I have heard some say that if they were to profess to have been filled with the Holy Ghost they would immediately expect their wings to appear. But such people are not likely to have wings in this world, or that which is to come. But in contrast to such notions as these, the early Church had lots of just such men as this beautiful man we call Barnabas, for we read that on the day of Pentecost they were all filled with the Holy Ghost. In fact the seven men that were selected by the early Church to look after its temporalities were all filled with the Holy Ghost. The fact is, beloved, that to be full of the Holy Ghost was the rule and not the exception. For nobody can read of the Church of that day and fail to see that as worshipers they had no idea of grinning at and sneering at and rejecting the Holy Ghost, and we believe from the very deep of our souls that it is the blood-bought privilege and the high vocation of every member of the Church to have this same blessed Holy Ghost to come into his heart and life, and flood every nook and corner of his soul, filling and thrilling us with this power divine, and imparting to each and all of us a degree of energy and unction and power that would make us mighty through God to the pulling down of the strongholds of sin and Satan about us.

There is no doubt in my mind about Barnabas having this spiritual energy, because his whole nature was possessed of God, and that imparted to him a boldness and courage and enthusiasm that made him a success wherever he went. The fact is, if we would become religious enthusiasts we must possess the same power and if we would have power over men we must have enthusiasm. No artist paints a great picture, and no poet produces a great poem, and no musician a great work without enthusiasm. It is also true that no Christian will make a successful worker without enthusiasm nor will the enthusiasm of humanity be enough, we must have the enthusiasm of divinity. Without this we will be cold and formal and calculative and will not get anywhere. It has been said that a bar of iron by itself is dead, but when it is magnetized, it will attract other bars, and will draw them to it and lift them and carry them about. So it will be with us, and so it was with Barnabas. If we are full of the Holy Ghost we are sure to draw and attract and hold others rather than alienate them.

We have often thought that too much is being made of the little trouble between St. Paul and Barnabas over John Mark that led to their separation. Dr. Adam Clarke says he can see neither anger nor ill will on either side. Paul, of course, was influenced by a great love of righteousness, and Barnabas on the other hand was actuated by a love for his own relatives, and perhaps he felt by showing a friendly Christian interest in him that he might make a man out of him, and thank the Lord he did, and so they separated, Paul choosing Silas as his companion, to travel as a colaborer and worker, and Barnabas chose Mark, his relative, to be his companion, and as Dr. W. B. Godbey, who has just been translated to his heavenly home, used to tell us that God wanted two missionary bands instead of one, so through the divine plan Paul and Barnabas had to be separated, but there was no sin in the separation. In fact, it proved to be a good thing as the later events show, for henceforth we see two streams of living water flowing, where in the past we only had one. Before their separation we had only one missionary band, while after their separation we had two.

Before their separation Paul and Barnabas were both required to hold one meeting, while as far as we can see John Mark and Silas were doing nothing that was worth while, but after the separation of Paul and Barnabas we now see Paul and Silas and Barnabas and Mark carrying on two great revivals at the same time, and by the separation of Paul and Barnabas Mark and Silas were both brought into the great army of the Lord. Now they became red-hot, second-blessing evangelists, and there were two heaven-born holiness bands moving through the country by divine order leaving a stream of holy fire wherever they went. From the fact that God blessed both Paul and Silas is a clear proof to my mind that the men did not have a fuss that was engendered or brought about through anger or unkind feelings for each other. For we afterward hear Paul speaking of Barnabas as his true yoke-fellow and the reader will remember that at one time Paul and Peter didn't agree and Paul said publicly that he withstood Peter to the face for Peter was to be blamed, and we find that they loved each other, for when Paul went to Jerusalem he stayed with Peter two weeks, and when Peter wrote about Paul he called him, "our beloved brother Paul."

But we must remember that those men were passing through Judaism to Christianity, and they couldn't agree on what they were to eat always, and in fact we have not gotten over all those things yet after nineteen hundred years of Christian activity. Some good people nowadays believe that if a man eats pork, or oysters, or catfish, that he is still under the dominion of the Devil, while other good people believe that you can eat anything that your stomach calls for and enjoy it and do good work for the Lord, and we will probably never all agree on the same thing.

Not long ago a good lady said to me, "Brother Robinson, how in the world can you drink coffee and profess to be sanctified?" I told the lady I would show her exactly how the thing was done, whereupon I took a cup of coffee and put a little cream in it and a spoonful of sugar and stirred it up and turned it up to my mouth and drank it in the presence of the lady, and I said to her, "Now, sister, that is exactly the way I do it." The reader will see at a glance that the lady asked me how it could be done, and I showed her the way the thing was pulled off.

Next we notice that Barnabas proved himself to be a successful evangelist. If you will follow him carefully through the records, you will see how God put His seal upon the ministry of this man. Aside from the good he would do to others in the way of material help and aside from the honor that came to him in being selected by the Church to oversee that work in Antioch because of his spiritual gifts and graces, and aside from the fact that he was also chosen to carry means of relief to the brethren which dwelt in Judea, we can not fail to see that winning souls was the chief joy, for right here in Antioch under his burning and fiery message we read that much people was added to the Lord. You will notice that the additions here were to the Lord, rather than to the church. You see there is a big difference between adding people to the church and adding them to the Lord. We fear that many people have been added to the church who were not first added to the Lord.

In this same city we read Paul and Barnabas remained a whole year, and it is said that they taught much people and the work was so genuine and the change wrought was so manifest, that the disciples were first called Christians in Antioch. Thank the Lord, that is the very city where Barnabas remained for a year. Then we read in Acts 13th chapter 5th verse that they came to Salamis and preached the Word in the synagogue of the Jews. They had also John to their ministry, and at Paphos, and Perga, and Antioch in Pisidia their preaching had a most transforming effect. We read in Acts 13th chapter 44th verse that almost the whole city came together to hear the Word of the Lord, and coming to Iconium it is said in Acts 14th chapter 1st verse that they so spake that a great multitude believed, both of the Jews and of the Greeks. Here we find that Barnabas preached such a wonderful gospel that he even turned multitudes to the Lord. That proves that Barnabas was a successful evangelist, and these two men preached in such a remarkable way here that they called Barnabas Jupiter and Paul Mercurius, because they thought the gods had come down to them in the likeness of men.

The reader will notice that there was a stream of victory and success that went with this man's beautiful life that remains until the present day. Barnabas never held a card-signing revival. When a man can preach the gospel with such power and enthusiasm that the multitudes will believe that he is a god come down from heaven, gentlemen, they are not able to sign cards. The revivals that were held by Barnabas were nothing short of old-fashioned, heart-felt, Holy Ghost revivals, that defeated the Devil and and robbed the pit and honored God and glorified Christ and populated heaven. The revivals held by Barnabas lasted after he had left town. How long this beautiful man continued his evangelistic campaign we are not told in the sacred Book, but we have read from the pen of some ancient writer that Barnabas finally went to the city of Milan, and he became the first bishop of the church in that city. Whether that is correct or not we know not, but we know he was capable of being anything to the church, and his beautiful life has left a good taste in the mouth of every New Testament reader. We don't know where he finished his days, but we do know that he is one man that died in the triumphs of a gospel faith and received the crown of righteousness, and that he will shine in the brightness of that celestial city forever and ever. May the Lord bless every reader of this little sketch of that beautiful man that we call Barnabas.

33

The Morning Glory and the Glory of the Morning

TWO NAMES SO MUCH alike and yet how different they often are! To illustrate, take the "morning glory," and the "glory of the morning." The morning glory is a beautiful little flower that blooms out on the little climbing vines that are often planted about the doors of our homes. The little vine will climb the twine string until it reaches the top of the porch and then the lovely little vine will cover the top of the porch, and they will hang in great clusters down over the doorway, and early in the morning while the dew is on the whole porch will be covered, and all kinds of lovely flowers, and as long as the morning stays cool and fresh, the flowers could not be more beautiful—all colors, red and white and blue and purple, dazzling in the early morning sunlight. But as soon as the dew dries off the morning glories are ready to drop from their tiny little stems, and wither up in the heat. But while the dew is on they are so lovely and so beautiful that somebody called them morning glories, and that lovely name got out on them. It has stuck to them like a postage stamp sticks to the envelope.

It would make me feel sad if the morning glories were called by some other name. When you see the morning glories in bloom you know that the dear Lord has been in the community, for no man could mix his colors to make the vine so dark and green and fresh, and yet red and white and purple, and oh, those dark blue ones, how they dance and shine in the morning sunlight! When I look at them I just want to run and jump right in the middle of the vine and get my arms full of those lovely little friends of mine, and plant a dozen kisses on their dainty little faces, and when they raise their tiny but beautiful little heads to heaven all damp with the morning dew, you just have to stop and look at them. They command you like so many commanding officers, and I just dare you to go by and not say, "Good morning, morning glories." If you love the Lord you will feel like taking off your hat to them, for you are in the presence of perfection and beauty and loveliness. They look like Jesus had spent the night with them. You feel that He had joined in with them and sung a morning lullaby, and had just given them a parting kiss, and had withdrawn just a little way, and was looking through the morning sunlight at a cluster of morning glories.

But there is a great difference between the morning glory and the glory of the morning. The glory of the morning is brought into display by the rising of the sun, as that fiery charger rolls up over the blue dome and shakes sparks of living fire from his outstretched wings, we stand in awe and are made to wonder at the glory of our God, the builder of the heavens and earth, and thank God, the Creator of the universe. How strange, how refreshing, how marvelous, how glorious! Are you surprised that this wonderful hour is called the morning? King Solomon said, "Who is this that looketh forth as the morning?"

Just watch that fiery chariot as he climbs the mountain peaks, and throws handfuls of morning light down into that valley. Do you wonder that the lambs are bleating and the birds are singing and the brooks are humming the morning tune? Do you wonder that the hens are cackling and the calves are bawling, and the pups are barking? Just listen as the girls play that organ. It sounds like a brand-new one. Listen to the boys in the back yard as they whoop and yell, as they stand on their feet one minute and their heads the next. What does it all mean? Why, man, this is the glory of the morning. Take another look and you will see mountains of floating clouds and they will smile on you as you wave them a happy good morning. But the next moment you will see what looks to be tons of granulated sugar and train loads of whipped cream, and you will feel like throwing your hat in the air and shouting to the top of your voice that the angels are having whipped cream for breakfast, and all nature joins in a great praise meeting.

And we just look up and say, "Glory to God! and hardly know why we said it. Well, we just had to say it, for it said itself, for that was your expression of the "glory of morning." But as we stand and gaze on the wonder of this glory we hear the humming of the bees and we see them out at the daybreak gathering honey from the clover blossoms and their little heads are wet with the morning dew as they have soused them through the dewdrops gathering their morning meal. Praise the Lord for the glory of the morning, and praise him for the morning glory, and praise the Lord for "*bees in the clover.*"

Don't miss these other great books by
the same author!

Honey in the Rock

Mountain Peaks

A Pitcher of Cream

Order direct from the publisher by calling toll free:

800-S$_7$P$_7$B$_2$O$_6$O$_6$K$_5$S$_7$

You may also order by writing:
Schmul Publishing Company
PO Box 716
Salem, OH 44460

Members of Schmul's Wesleyan Book
Club buy these outstanding books at
40% off the retail price!
It's like having a discount Christian bookstore in your mailbox!
In addition, buy any book already on our extensive list of
published titles at 40% off!

*Join Schmul's Wesleyan Book Club by
calling us toll-free:*

800-S₇P₇B₂O₆O₆K₅S₇

Put a discount Christian bookstore in your own mailbox.

You may also order direct from the publisher by writing:
Schmul Publishing Company
PO Box 716
Salem, OH 44460